TO:

Michael

FROM:

Uncle Tom & Aunt Joy

DATE:

Christmas 2023

May you embrace
Gods wisdom for your
life !

Wisdom
for
the Way

365 *Days of Wise Words*
for Busy People

Charles R. Swindoll

THOMAS NELSON
Since 1798

Published in Nashville, Tennessee, by Thomas Nelson. Thomas Nelson is a registered trademark of HarperCollins Christian Publishing, Inc.

Unless otherwise noted, Scripture quotations are taken from the Holy Bible, New Living Translation. Copyright © 1996, 2004, 2015 by Tyndale House Foundation. Used by permission of Tyndale House Ministries, Carol Stream, Illinois 60188. All rights reserved.

Scripture quotations marked AMPC are taken from the Amplified® Bible (AMPC). Copyright © 1954, 1958, 1962, 1964,1965, 1987 by The Lockman Foundation. Used by permission. www.Lockman.org.

Scripture quotations marked KJV are taken from the King James Version. Public domain.

Scripture quotations marked NASB are taken from the New American Standard Bible® (NASB). Copyright © 1960, 1962, 1963, 1968, 1971, 1972, 1973, 1975, 1977, 1995 by The Lockman Foundation. Used by permission. www.Lockman.org.

Scripture quotations marked NIV are taken from the Holy Bible, New International Version®, NIV®. Copyright © 1973, 1978, 1984, 2011 by Biblica, Inc.® Used by permission of Zondervan. All rights reserved worldwide. www.zondervan.com. The "NIV" and "New International Version" are trademarks registered in the United States Patent and Trademark Office by Biblica, Inc.®

Scripture quotations marked NKJV are taken from the New King James Version®. Copyright © 1982 by Thomas Nelson. Used by permission. All rights reserved.

Devotions referencing the Phillips translation are citing Scripture quotations taken from The New Testament in Modern English by J. B. Phillips. Copyright © 1960, 1972 J. B. Phillips. Administered by The Archbishops' Council of the Church of England. Used by permission.

Devotions referencing The Living Bible are citing Scripture quotations taken from The Living Bible. Copyright © 1971. Used by permission of Tyndale House Publishers, a Division of Tyndale House Ministries, Carol Stream, Illinois 60188. All rights reserved.

Any internet addresses, phone numbers, or company or product information printed in this book are offered as a resource and are not intended in any way to be or to imply an endorsement by Thomas Nelson, nor does Thomas Nelson vouch for the existence, content, or services of these sites, phone numbers, companies, or products beyond the life of this book.

ISBN 978-1-4002-3178-2

Printed in China

21 22 23 24 25 SKY 5 4 3 2 1

DEDICATION

It was my distinct honor and joy to serve as the president of Dallas Theological Seminary from 1994 to 2001. A major reason that adventure was such a delight is due, in part, to the pleasant relationship I sustained with the school's Board of Incorporate Members.

I dedicate this volume to that body of faithful men and women who gave such wise oversight to that outstanding institution. The title and contents of this book describe the kind of leadership they embodied. My life is deeper because of my time with them. May our Lord abundantly reward them for their selfless devotion and uncompromising integrity. My love and appreciation for each of them knows no bounds.

PREFACE

We have not even begun to live if we lack the wisdom God wants to give to us. That wisdom is ours, simply for the asking, and it brings us into a whole new and exciting world! Like birth, it will take time and it may be a painful process. But when it comes, you'll be amazed how clearly things will come into focus. You'll begin to feel like a new creature. No wonder Jesus referred to it as being "born again."

When we operate in the sphere of the wisdom of God, when it is at work in our minds and in our lives, we look at life through lenses of perception, and we respond to it in calm confidence. There's a remarkable absence of fear. We are not seized with panic. We can either lose our jobs or we can be promoted in our work, and neither will derail us.

Why? Because we see it with God-given objectivity. And we handle it in His wisdom. We can dip into an unexpected valley or we can soar to the pinnacle of prosperity, and we can cope with both extremes. His wisdom provides us the necessary objectivity and stability. This is not some dreamland fantasy. It is reality. It is the ability to live above the drag of human opinion and horizontal perspective. It is what happens within us when wisdom goes to work.

The wisdom of God gives us *balance, strength*, and *insight*. None of these is a natural trait; each is a by-product of wisdom. We don't get these things just because we're human beings. They must come from God.

But the more we glean God's wisdom, the more strength we gain to live with questions and tension. He doesn't issue rules and regulations for every moment. He provides some overall guidelines and principles, and then He allows us to make the decisions. Why? By doing this the wisdom of God goes to work, and we begin to learn how to walk through life—which is often full of subtle and unseen "land mines." His wisdom provides the sixth sense we need. It matures us so that we can press on in spite of the unanswered questions.

The good news is that such wisdom is ours to claim through an intimate relationship with God's Son, Jesus. He is the channel through which wisdom comes to us. In coming by faith to the Lord Jesus Christ, we are given open access to the wisdom of God. With the Son of God comes the wisdom of God. It's all part of the package.

Pastor Charles R. Swindoll

JANUARY

NO SUCCESS WITHOUT WISDOM

That's the value of wisdom; it helps you succeed.
ECCLESIASTES 10:10

I don't know of a hotter subject today than success. Magazine articles, books, seminars, and sermons promote it. But success is seldom linked with wisdom. Chances are good that if we would pick up last Sunday's paper and read it through, we'd come across twenty or more references to success, yet find nothing added regarding wisdom. In today's hype about success, wisdom is conspicuous by its absence. Outside of biblical literature and biblically based books, we hardly even come across the word. . . .

[Wisdom] may not give us great popularity and wealth, and it may not mean that we will be the most respected in our field or that we will have the most significant voice in the company, but ultimately, as God gauges it, we will be successful.

Living on the Ragged Edge

In your life, when have you succeeded because of wisdom?

_____

_____

_____

_____

THE ABCs OF LOVE

Hatred stirs up quarrels, but love makes up for all offenses.
PROVERBS 10:12

I accept you as you are."
"I believe you are valuable."
"I care when you hurt."
"I desire only what is best for you."
"I erase all offenses."

We could call that the ABCs of love. And I don't know of anybody who would turn his back on such magnetic, encouraging statements.

There is nothing shallow about authentic love. Nor is it a magic wand we whip out and wave over a problem with a whoosh, hoping all the pain will go away. Real love has staying power. Authentic love is tough love. It refuses to look for ways to run away. It always opts for working through. It doesn't cop out because the sea gets stormy and rough. It's fibrous and resilient. . . . While the world around us gives the opposite counsel, love stands firm.

Dropping Your Guard

When have you been shown authentic love?

_____

_____

_____

REAL RICHES

In [Christ] lie hidden all the treasures of wisdom and knowledge.
COLOSSIANS 2:3

From the looks of things, you're pretty impressive. You've got a nice place. And I suppose your neighbors would agree that you're a hard worker . . . climbing right on up that ladder toward success, right?

Your salary is good and your material possessions are growing in number, but . . . the truth is you are empty on the inside and you're faking it on the outside. Not one thing you own in your "kingdom" has brought you the happiness you long for. So you're thinking, "Maybe if I could land that better job," or "get into that bigger house," or . . . or . . .

But don't allow the smoke screen of more money to blind your eyes to the truth. There's a lot more to being rich than making more money. Seneca, the Roman, was right: "Money has never yet made anyone rich." Do you want riches? Then listen to Jesus: "But seek first His kingdom and His righteousness, and all these things will be provided to you" (Matthew 6:33 NASB).

For the real riches, try switching kingdoms.

Living on the Ragged Edge

What do you believe makes you rich? Has your belief changed through the years?

_____

_____

POWER TO OVERCOME

Commit yourself to instruction; listen carefully to words of knowledge.
PROVERBS 23:12

Can't and won't. Christians need to be very careful which one they choose. It seems that we prefer to use "can't."

"I just can't get along with my wife."

"My husband and I can't communicate."

"I just can't discipline the kids as I should."

"I just can't give up the affair I'm having."

"I can't stop overeating."

"I can't find time to pray."

Any Christian who takes the Bible seriously will have to agree the word here really should be "won't." Why? Because we have been given the power, the ability to overcome.

We're really saying, "I won't," because we don't choose to say, "With the help of God, I will!"

Day by Day with Charles Swindoll

In what areas of your life can you change your dialogue from **I won't** to **I will with God's help**?

_____

_____

_____

GOD'S PLAN FOR HOPE

"For I know the plans I have for you," says the Lord. "They are plans for good and not for disaster, to give you a future and a hope."

JEREMIAH 29:11

God knows, right down to the final nub, exactly where you are in life. He sees. He cares. He is aware. And best of all, He is touched by it.

The enemy of our souls wants you to think differently. *God doesn't care. He's left you in this mess for so many months. How unfair! Those around you, those at work, your neighbors, live like the devil, and they're making it fine. And here you don't even have a job. You don't even have enough to cover the credit card bills. What kind of God is that?*

Or maybe some young mother-to-be, stretched to the limit already with other young children and crushing responsibilities, cries out in her heart, "My situation is more than I can bear!" And God replies, "My daughter, I know what I am doing. I know the pain of your heart right now. I know you feel overwhelmed, overloaded, pressed down. But believe Me, I am touched by your situation. And I have a plan! I am working out the details of your deliverance even now. Trust Me!"

Moses: A Man of Selfless Dedication

When has God come through for you during a difficult situation? When have you seen Him come through for others?

_____

_____

FIVE CHEERS FOR MOM

She carefully watches everything in her household. . . . Her
children stand and bless her. Her husband praises her.
PROVERBS 31:27–28

What does motherhood require? Transparent tenderness, authentic spirituality, inner confidence, unselfish love, and self-control. Quite a list, isn't it? Almost more than we should expect. Perhaps that explains why Erma Bombeck used to say that motherhood takes 180 movable parts and 3 pairs of hands and 3 sets of eyes . . . and, I might add, the grace of God. If you happen to be a mother, here's one guy who applauds your every effort. Five cheers for all you do!

Remember the Skin Horse in *The Velveteen Rabbit*? All his stuffing was starting to come out, his hair had been "loved off," but how valuable he was! Carefully kept mothers don't have secure kids. Carefully kept, untouchable "velveteen mothers" turn out fragile, selfish, untouchable children. But unselfish, giving, secure moms somehow manage to deposit healthy, wholesome kids into our lonely, frightened society.

Growing Wise in Family Life

What characteristics do you see in mothers you admire? How can you incorporate these qualities into your own life?

_____

_____

GOD'S NEW MORNING MESSAGE

The Lord lifts up those who are weighed down. The Lord loves the godly.

PSALM 146:8

D o you know what God's fresh, new morning message is to us? Whether the sun is shining brightly or whether it's pouring down rain? Whether the morning is bright or whether it's gray and overcast? His promise is the dawn itself. Every morning the Lord comes through with His encouraging message, "We're still on speaking terms, you know! I'm here. I haven't moved. Let's go together today."

Trust God to remember you. He won't forget your name. He won't forget your circumstances. He certainly won't forget your prayers. Trust Him; He remembers you.

The Mystery of God's Will

Why not start a conversation with God **right now**? He's listening. What would you like to say to Him?

_____

_____

_____

_____

_____

NO FEAR OF FAILURE

The wicked run away when no one is chasing them,
but the godly are as bold as lions.
PROVERBS 28:1

When will we ever learn that there are no hopeless situations, only people who have grown hopeless about them? What appears as an unsolvable problem to us is actually a rather exhilarating challenge. People who inspire others are those who see invisible bridges at the end of dead-end streets.

There was a cabinet meeting in London during the darkest days of the Second World War. France had just capitulated. Prime Minister Churchill outlined the situation in its starkest colors. Quite literally, the tiny British Isles stood alone. Grim faces stared back at him in stoic silence. Despair and thoughts of surrender were written in their looks. The visionary statesman momentarily remained silent, lit a cigar, showed a hint of a smile, and with a twinkle in his eye, responded to that dispirited company of officials, "Gentlemen, I find it rather inspiring." What a great line! No wonder people followed the man. Fear of failure never entered his mind!

Dropping Your Guard

Whom do you find inspiring and courageous? How do their actions embolden you to face challenges?

_____

_____

A LOVING FATHER

Happy are those who hear the joyful call to worship, for
they will walk in the light of your presence, Lord.
Psalm 89:15

God doesn't sit in heaven with His jaws clenched, His arms folded in disapproval, and a deep frown on His brow. He is not ticked off at His children for all the times we trip over our tiny feet and fall flat on our diapers. He is a loving Father, and we are precious in His sight, the delight of His heart. After all, He "has qualified us to share in the inheritance of the saints in light" (Colossians 1:12 NASB). Think of it! He's put us in His inheritance!

Remember that the next time you think God is coming down on you. You have reason to give thanks. You don't have to qualify yourself for His kingdom. His grace has rescued you.

Hope Again

When has God shown His love for you? When have you seen it shown in the lives of others?

_____

_____

_____

_____

PRECEPTS AND PRINCIPLES

I believe in your commands; now teach me good judgment and knowledge.
PSALM 119:66

Whenever you see the scriptural phrase "This is the will of God," you know for sure that's God's will. You also know that to disobey is to break His Word. Other clear indications of His leading are the precepts and principles in Scripture.

Precepts are clearly marked statements like "Abstain from sexual immorality." That's like saying, "Speed Limit 35." What is speeding? Anything more than thirty-five miles an hour. That's a precept.

Then there are principles . . . and these are general guidelines that require discernment and maturity if we are to grasp them. Like the sign that says, "Drive carefully." This may mean forty miles an hour on a clear, uncongested highway, or it may mean ten miles an hour on an ice-covered curve. But it always means that we must be alert and aware of conditions; it always means we have to be discerning. These principles require wisdom and discernment.

The Mystery of God's Will

What precepts and principles in the Bible do you find yourself returning to often?

_____

_____

FRIENDLY PEOPLE, THOUGHTFUL PEOPLE

A real friend sticks closer than a brother.

PROVERBS 18:24

If I have learned anything during my journey on planet Earth, it is that people need one another. The presence of other people is essential—caring people, helpful people, interesting people, friendly people, thoughtful people. These folks take the grind out of life. About the time we are tempted to think we can handle things all alone—*boom*! We run into some obstacle and need assistance. We discover all over again that we are not nearly as self-sufficient as we thought.

In spite of our high-tech world and efficient procedures, people remain the essential ingredient of life. When we forget that, a strange thing happens: we start treating people like inconveniences instead of assets.

Laugh Again

Who are the friendly, thoughtful people in your life? How have they enhanced your life?

_____

_____

_____

_____

DON'T GET BURNED!

Bad company corrupts good character.
1 CORINTHIANS 15:33

Compromise never works. We always get burned. Even though we rationalize around our weak decisions and tell ourselves that wicked associations really won't harm us ("They'll get better; our good will rub off their bad!"), we get soiled in the process.

If you put on a pair of clean white gloves on a rainy day and then go out into the backyard to the flower bed and pick up a glob of mud, trust me, the mud will never get "glovey." The gloves will definitely get muddy. Every time. In all my years on earth, I have never seen glovey mud. Not once. In simple terms, that's what 1 Corinthians 15:33 is saying: "Do not be deceived: 'Bad company corrupts good morals'" (NASB).

Dropping Your Guard

Was there a time when you realized you were in bad company and changed your situation? What good did that change produce?

_____

_____

_____

_____

PULL IN THE ANCHOR

"Forgive us our sins, as we have forgiven those who sin against us."
MATTHEW 6:12

Have you done someone wrong? Have you been offensive? Have your actions caused hurt? To do nothing is not only in direct disobedience to Jesus' teaching, it also complicates your life. It adds heavier mental weights than you are capable of carrying. It is like dropping an anchor and then cranking up your boat's engine and putting it in gear. The anchor keeps catching and snagging on the bottom, making for a terribly uncomfortable ride across the water. How simple the solution! Just pull in the anchor.

Let me give you a simple tip: we cannot be right with God until we are right with others.

Simple Faith

How has forgiveness—either extended by you or given to you—changed the course of your life?

_____

_____

_____

_____

SEGMENTS OF SOLITUDE

Let all that I am wait quietly before God, for my hope is in him.
PSALM 62:5

An insightful author once called solitude the "furnace of transformation." This doesn't refer to mere personal privacy for a twelve-second pit stop where we get a quick fix to reenter the race. It's more than that. It's an oasis of the soul where we see ourselves, others, and especially our God in new ways. It's where much of the "clutter" of life is identified and exterminated, thanks to the merciless heat of the "furnace." Soul surgery transpires as serenity replaces anxiety.

In solitude, struggles occur that no one else knows about. Inner battles are fought here that seldom become fodder for sermons or illustrations for books. God, who probes our deepest thoughts during protracted segments of solitude, opens our eyes to things that need attention. It is here He makes us aware of those things we try to hide from others.

Intimacy with the Almighty

When has God shined a light on the areas of your life where you needed attention? How did He start healing you in those places?

_____

_____

_____

GOD'S HAND ON YOUR LIFE

You watched me as I was being formed in utter seclusion,
as I was woven together in the dark of the womb.
PSALM 139:15

Perhaps you never knew what it was to nestle securely in a parent's love. Your home life may have been strained or even fractured from your earliest memory. From a human point of view, your birth might have come at a difficult or awkward time in your parents' lives. It may be that you've never known the reassurance of a faithful mother and father who built their faith into your heart. When you think back on your growing-up years, you realize you don't have much to shout about.

I'd like to deliver a beautiful message to you, my friend. God's hand on your life may be just beginning to make its mark. That steep hill you've been climbing for such a long time may be the ramp to a destiny beyond your dreams. I do not believe there is any such thing as an accidental or ill-timed birth. You may have arrived in a home that was financially strapped. You may have known brokenness, hurt, and insecurity since your earliest days—but please hear me on this: *You were not an accident.*

Moses: A Man of Selfless Dedication

How do you feel knowing that God has a hand on your life?

_____

_____

GIVING GOD FIRST PLACE

For whoever finds [wisdom] finds life and receives favor from the LORD.
PROVERBS 8:35

I f some corporate position is the god of your life, then something terrible occurs within when it is no longer a future possibility. If your career, however, is simply a part of God's plan and you keep it in proper perspective, you can handle a demotion just as well as you can handle a promotion. It all depends on who's first and what's first.

Breaking the magnet that draws things ahead of God is a lengthy and sometimes painful process. There is a line found in the Jewish Talmud that puts it well: "Man is born with his hands clenched; he dies with them wide open. Entering life, he desires to grasp everything; leaving the world, all he possessed has slipped away."

Just remember: whatever is in first place, if it isn't Christ alone, it is in the wrong place.

Living Above the Level of Mediocrity

Has there been a time when you realized God wasn't first in your life? How did you change your priorities?

_____

_____

_____

ALONE WITH GOD

*This is what the Sovereign LORD ... says: "In
quietness and confidence is your strength."*
ISAIAH 30:15

S ome of the most profound ministries of the Spirit of God are not public or
loud or large. Sometimes His most meaningful touch on our lives comes
when we are all alone.

I urge you to include in your schedule time to be alone with God. You do
have places where you can get away for a long walk, don't you? I hope it's in
a wooded area. The gentle breeze blowing through the forest is therapeutic.
Sometimes just being alone out in God's marvelous creation is all that's needed
for the scales to be removed from your eyes and for you to silence the harass-
ment and the noise of your day and begin to hear from God.

Flying Closer to the Flame

Where do you like to go to be alone and spend time with God?

_____

_____

_____

_____

_____

IT IS FINISHED

For everyone has sinned; we all fall short of God's glorious standard.
Yet God, in his grace, freely makes us right in his sight. He did this
through Christ Jesus when he freed us from the penalty for our sins.
ROMANS 3:23–24

Stop and think: Upon believing in Jesus Christ's substitutionary death and bodily resurrection, the once-lost sinner is instantly, unconditionally, and permanently declared 100 percent righteous. Anything less and we are not righteous. . . . We're *almost* righteous.

If we are declared 99.9 percent righteous, some verses of the Bible would have to be rewritten. Like Isaiah 1:18, which might then read: "Come now, and let us reason together," says the Lord, "though your sins are as scarlet, they will be light pink."

Nonsense! The promise of sins forgiven is all or nothing. Eighty percent won't cut it.

When our Lord said, "It is finished" (John 19:30), He meant "finished."

The Finishing Touch

How do you feel knowing you are 100 percent forgiven and 100 percent righteous?

_____

_____

_____

TWO ARE BETTER THAN ONE

Two people are better off than one, for they can help each other succeed.

ECCLESIASTES 4:9

Independence is our watchword and "Think for Yourself" is our motto. Declaring a need is a sign of weakness, an open admission of failure and lack of character. Furthermore, we are on the move so much, who has time to share and to care? It has been my observation that we Christians are not immune from this hurry-up, hassle-hustle mentality.

Even though it is easy to buy into the selfish lifestyle and opt for isolationism instead of involvement, the consequences are bitter and inescapable. Swimming with the current of today's me-ism mindset has a way of eclipsing the contrasting light of Scripture.

Two are better than one because:

- they have a good return for their labor—*mutual effort*
- one will lift up his companion—*mutual support*
- they keep each other warm—*mutual encouragement*
- they can resist an attack—*mutual strength*

Dropping Your Guard

When in your life have you needed help or support and found that two are better than one?

_____

_____

HONEST TO THE CORE

Obey my commands and live! Guard my instructions as you guard your own eyes.
PROVERBS 7:2

What is God looking for? He is looking for men and women whose hearts are completely His—*completely.*

God is not looking for magnificent specimens of humanity. He's looking for deeply spiritual, genuinely humble, honest-to-the-core servants who have integrity.

Today we live in a world that says, in many ways, "If you just make a good impression, that's all that matters." But you will never be a man or woman of God if that's your philosophy. Never. You cannot fake it with the Almighty. He is not impressed with externals. He always focuses on the inward qualities . . . those things that take time and discipline to cultivate.

David: A Man of Passion and Destiny

In what ways can you serve God with an honest and whole heart?

_____

_____

_____

_____

_____

A WELL-CHOSEN WORD

Timely advice is lovely, like golden apples in a silver basket.
PROVERBS 25:11

Like Jell-O, concepts assume the mold of the words into which they are poured. Who has not been stabbed awake by the use of a particular word . . . or combination of words? Who has not found relief from a well-timed word spoken at the precise moment of need? Who has not been crushed beneath the weight of an ill-chosen word? And who has not gathered fresh courage because a word of hope penetrated the fog of self-doubt? The term *word* remains the most powerful of all four-letter words.

Colors fade.

Shorelines erode.

Temples crumble. Empires fall. But "a word fitly spoken" (Proverbs 25:11 KJV) endures.

Simple Faith

When have words spoken to you helped you heal through a situation? When have they uplifted and encouraged you?

_____

_____

_____

_____

THE SECRET IS ACCEPTANCE

"I will put my trust in him."
HEBREWS 2:13

Helen Roseveare was a British medical missionary in the Congo years ago during an uprising. Her faith was strong and her trust was confident, yet she was raped and assaulted and treated brutally. Commenting later, she said, "I must ask myself a question as if it came directly from the Lord. 'Can you thank Me for trusting you with this experience even if I never tell you why?'"

What a profound thought. God has trusted each of us with our own set of unfair circumstances and unexplained experiences to deal with. Can we still trust in Him even if He never tells us why?

The secret to responsible trust is *acceptance*. Acceptance is taking from God's hand absolutely anything He gives, looking into His face in trust and with thanksgiving, knowing that the confinement of the hedge we're in is good and for His glory.

Perfect Trust

What experience have you learned to accept by trusting that God's plan is always good?

_____

_____

_____

DANGEROUS DISILLUSIONMENT

You will keep in perfect peace all who trust in you,
all whose thoughts are fixed on you!
ISAIAH 26:3

Disillusionment is a dangerous, slippery slope. First we become disillusioned about our fellow man. Then we move on to cynicism. Before long, we trust no one, not even God. We've been burned. We've been taken advantage of; we've been mistreated.

The cause of disillusionment and the cure for it can be expressed in almost the same simple words. The cause of disillusionment is *putting one's complete hope and trust in people.* Putting people on a pedestal, focusing on them, finding our security in them. And when the feet of clay crumble (as they surely will) total disillusionment sets in.

What's the cure? *Putting our complete hope and trust in the living Lord.* When we do that, the simplest messages from God calm our spirits.

Joseph: A Man of Integrity and Forgiveness

When did you shift your trust in people to trust in God? How did it change your perception of the people and the world around you?

_____

_____

_____

HEAVENLY HINDSIGHT

For you are my hiding place; you protect me from trouble.
You surround me with songs of victory.
PSALM 32:7

Providence. We toss the word around. But have you ever analyzed it? It comes from the Latin, *providentia*. *Pro* means "before" or "ahead of time"; *videntia* is from *videre*, meaning "to see." Put them together and you have "seeing ahead of time," which is what almighty God does. He sees the events of life ahead of time—something that we of course can never do.

We're great at history. Our hindsight is almost always 20/20. But we're lousy at prophecy, that is, the specifics of the future. Stop and think. We've no clue as to what will happen one minute from now, no idea what's going to happen next. But our invisible God, in His *providentia*, is continually, constantly, and confidently at work.

He never changes. He knows what He is about, and He pursues it with relentless determination.

Esther: A Woman of Strength and Dignity

Have you ever caught yourself acting as though you could predict the future? How did you learn to trust God and to let Him guide instead?

_____

_____

_____

CHECKING UP ON YOUR JOB

Lazy people want much but get little, but those who work hard will prosper.

PROVERBS 13:4

A young fellow rushed into a gas station to use the pay phone. The manager overheard his telephone conversation as he asked, "Sir, could you use a hardworking, honest young man to work for you?" [pause] "Oh . . . you've already got a hardworking, honest young man? Well, thanks anyway!"

The boy hung up the phone with a smile. Humming to himself, he began to walk away, obviously happy.

"How can you be so cheery?" asked the eavesdropping manager. "I thought the man you talked to already had someone and didn't want to hire you."

The young fellow answered, "Well, you see I *am* the hardworking young man. I was just checking up on my job!"

If you called your Boss, disguised your voice, and asked about your job, what do you think would be His answer?

Living Beyond the Daily Grind

How would God describe you? Would He say you're doing a good job?

_____

_____

_____

_____

MORAL CHARACTER

Choose a good reputation over great riches; being held
in high esteem is better than silver or gold.
PROVERBS 22:1

U nfortunately, we have grown accustomed to shrugging off lapses in moral character, manifested in secretive and deceptive lifestyles. We are frequently told that trying to find people who value honesty and model responsibility, who promote fairness, accountability, loyalty, respect for others, and who hold to strong, upright convictions is not at all realistic.

"Such people don't exist. . . . We need to stop requiring personal purity," we are told. Or, as one airheaded soul said during a presidential campaign, "We're voting for president, not pope."

To such an analogy, I reply, "Nonsense!" That kind of logic (or rather, lack of logic) gives me the jitters.

Day by Day with Charles Swindoll

Who in your life displays honorable moral character? Would people in your life describe you this way? Why or why not?

_____

_____

_____

_____

CELEBRATE LIFE!

Teach us to realize the brevity of life, so that we may grow in wisdom.
PSALM 90:12

The Hebrew text suggests that we correctly "account" for our days. I find it interesting that we are to view life by the days, not *the years*. We are to live those days in such a way that when they draw to a close, we have gained "a heart of wisdom" (Psalm 90:12 NASB). With the Lord God occupying first place in our lives, we accept and live each day enthusiastically for Him. The result will be that "heart of wisdom" the psalmist mentioned.

Because we cannot alter the inevitable, we adjust to it. And we do that not a year at a time, but a day at a time. Instead of eating our heart out because a few more aches and pains have attached themselves to our bodies, we determine to celebrate life rather than endure it. Aging isn't a choice. But our response to it is. In so many ways we ourselves determine how we shall grow old.

Strengthening Your Grip

What small things can you do every day to ensure you are celebrating life and living enthusiastically for God?

_____

_____

_____

_____

GOD'S INSTRUCTION BOOK

And we know that the Son of God has come, and he has given
us understanding so that we can know the true God.
1 JOHN 5:20

God offers instruction, but then it's our move. We must accept His instruction and apply it to our lives. Then, and only then, can we expect to cash in on the benefits of His instruction. So you see, application is the essential link between instruction and change.

God has sent us His instruction. He has preserved every word of it in a book, the Bible. It's all there, just as He communicated it to us. When He returns for His own, He isn't going to ask us how much we memorized or how often we met for study. No, He will want to know, "What did you do about My instructions?"

Living Above the Level of Mediocrity

How are you living a life that shows you are following God's instructions?

_____

_____

_____

_____

_____

_____

GIVE GOD YOUR WORRIES

Who among you fears the LORD? . . . Trust in the LORD and rely on your God.
ISAIAH 50:10

Let's get six words clearly fixed in our minds. These six words form the foundation of God's therapeutic process for all worrywarts: *Worry about nothing; pray about everything.*

What qualifies as a worry? Anything that drains your tank of joy—something you cannot change, something you are not responsible for, something you are unable to control, something (or someone) that frightens and torments you, agitates you, keeps you awake when you should be asleep. All of that now needs to be switched from your worry list to your prayer list. Give each worry—one by one—to God. Tell Him you will no longer keep your anxiety to yourself.

The more you practice giving your mental burdens to the Lord, the more exciting it gets to see how God will handle the things that are impossible for you to do anything about.

Laugh Again

What worries in your life do you need to give to God in prayer?

_____

_____

_____

_____

THE SWEET TASTE OF SUCCESS?

Trust in your money and down you go! But the
godly flourish like leaves in spring.
PROVERBS 11:28

Our society has gorged itself on the sweet taste of success. We've filled our plates from a buffet of books that range from dressing for success to investing for success. We've gobbled down stacks of notebooks, audiobooks, and podcasts in our hunger for greater success.

The irony of all this is that . . . instead of fulfillment, we experience the bloated sensation of being full of ourselves—*our* dreams, *our* goals, *our* plans, *our* projects, *our* accomplishments. The result of this all-you-can-eat appetite is not contentment. It's nausea.

Hope Again

How can you ensure you are amassing those things that will not rust or decay? How are you storing up treasures in your heart rather than in your home?

_____

_____

_____

_____

FREE OF STRESS

O my people, trust in him at all times. Pour out
your heart to him, for God is our refuge.
PSALM 62:8

You and I could name things, specific things that we've gone through in the last several years that make no logical sense whatsoever. . . . But that's okay. We can't figure them out. But let me assure you: God is at work doing His mysterious plan (mysterious to us), which defies human logic. So quit trying to make it humanly logical. Trust Him.

Do you realize what a peaceful life you can live if you decide to live like this? Do you realize how relaxed you can be, how free of stress? Honestly. It's so helpful for me to remind myself: He is the One who is unfathomable. He is unsearchable. I'm neither.

The Mystery of God's Will

What small steps can you make every day toward fully trusting God's plan? How can you stop trying to "figure it out" and simply trust?

_____

_____

_____

_____

FEBRUARY

NO ISLAND OF SECOND CHANCES

Grandchildren are the crowning glory of the aged;
parents are the pride of their children.
PROVERBS 17:6

We cannot change the past. . . . And that includes the way we reared our children. All of us—yes, every parent I have ever met—would love to step into the time machine and go to the Island of Second Chances. We would give anything to relive those years and correct the failures and mistakes we committed the first time around. All such fantasy wishes need to be erased. They can never be fulfilled! The parenting process offers only one try per child, one day at a time, never again to be repeated.

Someone once said, "Life is like a coin; you can spend it any way you wish, but you spend it only once." That is never truer than with rearing children. About the time we get fairly good at it, our kids are all young adults and gone. Having come closer than ever to perfecting the process, we suddenly realize nobody is listening! Which means we're qualified for one major role: grandparenting (when it becomes our right to break all the rules and spoil those darlings!). It's a funny world.

Growing Wise in Family Life

What parenting regrets from past days do you need to release? How can you instead use what you have learned to help the next generation of parents?

_____

_____

A Fruitful Life

So we have not stopped praying for you. . . . Then the way you live will always honor and please the Lord, and your lives will produce every kind of good fruit.
COLOSSIANS 1:9–10

H ave you ever been in an area of the country where there was a lot of fruit ripening in the sun? Maybe on some cool September morning you've taken a walk through the apple orchards of the Hood River Valley, or along the Columbia River in Oregon. It is pleasing to the eye to see such an abundance of sweet, delicious fruit hanging on branch or vine, ready to be plucked.

A fruitful Christian life is like that—sweet, refreshing, nourishing, fragrant, sustaining, delightful to be near. But such a life requires careful cultivation. . . . A deeper, more consistent walk with Christ requires time and attention every day. If that happens, you will bear fruit.

Moses: A Man of Selfless Dedication

Who do you know whose life bears the fruit of the Spirit? What habits or practices does that person have in place that make them fruitful?

_____

_____

_____

_____

FULL OF GRACE AND TRUTH

God's unfailing love and faithfulness came through Jesus Christ.
JOHN 1:17

While thinking back on his days with Jesus, John (one of the Twelve) remembers there was something about Him that was like no one else, during which time His disciples "beheld His glory" (John 1:14 NKJV). His uniqueness was that incredible "glory," a glory that represented the very presence of God. In addition, this glorious One was "full of grace and truth." Pause and let that sink in. It was His glory mixed with grace and truth that made Him different. In a world of darkness and demands, rules and regulations, requirements and expectations demanded by hypocritical religious leaders, Jesus came and ministered in a new and different way—He alone, full of grace and full of truth, introduced a revolutionary, different way of life.

Remembering that uniqueness, John adds, "For of His fullness we have all received, and grace upon grace" (John 1:16 NASB).

The Grace Awakening

How does the grace and truth found in Jesus change the way you live? Are grace and truth evident in your life?

_____

_____

_____

"Good Job!"

How precious are your thoughts about me, O God. They cannot be numbered!
PSALM 139:17

Most of us are good at criticizing ourselves and finding fault with what we have done or failed to do. I'd like to suggest an alternate plan—spend some of your leisure time finding pleasure and satisfaction in what you have done as well as in who and what you are. Sound too liberal? Why? Since when is a good self-esteem liberal?

There are times we need to tell ourselves, "Good job!" when we know that is true. That isn't conceited pride, my friend. It's acknowledging in words the feelings of the heart. The Lord knows that we hear more than enough internal put-downs! Communicating in times of leisure includes self-affirmation, acknowledging, of course, that God ultimately gets the glory. After all, He's the One who makes the whole experience possible.

Strengthening Your Grip

What God-given gifts and talents do you possess? How often do you take the time to acknowledge all of the good that the Lord placed within you?

_____

_____

_____

_____

SAVOR SATISFACTION

Getting wisdom is the wisest thing you can do! And whatever else you do, develop good judgment.

PROVERBS 4:7

The good life—the one that truly satisfies—exists only when we stop wanting a better one. It is the condition of savoring what *is* rather than longing for what might be. The itch for things, the lust for more—so brilliantly injected by those who peddle them—is a virus draining our souls of happy contentment. Have you noticed? A man never earns enough. A woman is never beautiful enough. Clothes are never fashionable enough. Cars are never nice enough. Gadgets are never modern enough. Houses are never furnished enough. Food is never fancy enough. Relationships are never romantic enough. Life is never full enough.

Satisfaction comes when we step off the escalator of desire and say, "This is enough. What I have will do. What I make of it is up to me and my vital union with the living Lord."

Moses: A Man of Selfless Dedication

What small steps can you make every day toward fully trusting God's plan? How can you stop trying to "figure it out" and simply trust?

_____

_____

_____

MONEY CAN'T BUY EVERYTHING

How much better to get wisdom than gold, and good judgment than silver!
PROVERBS 16:16

Foolish indeed is the person who considers himself safe and sound because he has money.

And another reason it's foolish to trust in riches for security is that money, in the final analysis, brings no lasting satisfaction, certainly not in the area of things that really matter. There are many things that no amount of money can buy. It's been said that:

- Money can buy medicine, but not health.
- Money can buy a house, but not a home.
- Money can buy companionship, but not friends.
- Money can buy food, but not an appetite.
- Money can buy a bed, but not sleep.
- Money can buy the good life, but not eternal life.

It is God (alone) who is able to supply us with "all things to enjoy" (1 Timothy 6:17 KJV). As Seneca the Roman statesman once said: "Money has never yet made anyone rich."

Strengthening Your Grip

Where do you find the most joy and satisfaction in life? In what ways has the Lord made you rich?

_____

_____

GOD INCOMPREHENSIBLE!

Holy, holy, holy is the LORD of Heaven's Armies!
The whole earth is filled with his glory!
ISAIAH 6:3

What are the benefits of realizing God Incomprehensible? We no longer reduce Him to manageable terms. We are no longer tempted to manipulate Him and His will . . . or defend Him and His ways. Like the grieving prophet, we get new glimpses of Him "lofty and exalted," (Isaiah 6:1 NASB) surrounded by legions of seraphim who witness Him as "LORD of hosts" (v. 3 KJV) as they shout forth His praises in antiphonal voice (vv. 2–3 NASB).

In a world consumed with thoughts of itself, filled with people impressed with each other, having disconnected with the only One worthy of praise, it's time we return to Theology 101 and sit silently in His presence. It's time we catch a fresh glimpse of Him who, alone, is awesome—incomprehensible.

Day by Day with Charles Swindoll

Do you believe that God's ways and thoughts are higher than man's ways and thoughts? What if you viewed this truth not as a problem, but as a thing to be praised?

_____

_____

_____

_____

SUNRISE, SUNSET

Wisdom and money can get you almost anything,
but only wisdom can save your life.
ECCLESIASTES 7:12

God has given mankind the ability to see beyond the present. And He has not given that ability to any other creation. He has given us eternity in our hearts, without which "mankind will find out the work which God has done from the beginning even to *the end*" (Ecclesiastes 3:11 NASB).

I have italicized "the end" for the sake of emphasis. Let me tell you why. It doesn't take a lot of brains to realize that if there is a sunrise, there must also be a sunset. To borrow from the astronaut's word, if there is an "earthrise," there must also be an "earthset."

So let's take that one step further. If there is an earth beginning, there must also be an earth ending. And if I'm existing on this boring earth without God, then I'm certainly not ready for an earth ending when I must face the One who made me.

Living on the Ragged Edge

How are you spending your moments on earth? Are you living each day in a way that prepares you to stand before God in the end?

_____

_____

_____

THE WEIGHT OF WORRY

Give all your worries and cares to God, for he cares about you.
1 PETER 5:7

How wonderful that God personally cares about those things that worry us and prey upon our thoughts. He cares about them more than we care about them. Not a single nagging, aching, worrisome, stomach-tensing, blood-pressure-raising thought escapes His notice.

This is how the Phillips translation renders 1 Peter 5:7: "You can throw the whole weight of your anxieties upon him, for you are his personal concern."

Isn't that good? He genuinely cares. He is able to bear all the weight of your worry. Because you are His personal concern, you never disappear from His radar screen.

Moses: A Man of Selfless Dedication

Can you imagine the freedom of casting all your worries on God? How would you live this very day if you didn't have a worry in the world?

_____

_____

_____

_____

_____

REACH OUT TO OTHERS

The generous will prosper; those who refresh others will themselves be refreshed.
PROVERBS 11:25

Close, open relationships are vital. A glib "Hi, how are ya?" must be replaced with genuine concern. The key term is *connection*. When I use the word here, I'm referring to people reaching out to one another.

Being absorbed in the function of the family of God as a participant (rather than a spectator) means . . .

. . . relating to,

. . . working with,

. . . and caring for others whom I know and love.

As I read it over, I see written between the lines the reminder: This is not automatic. I am personally responsible. So are you!

Dropping Your Guard

Do you tend to settle for superficial relationships? What steps can you take to begin developing deeper connections with those around you?

_____

_____

_____

_____

_____

WONDERFULLY MADE

*Thank you for making me so wonderfully complex! Your
workmanship is marvelous—how well I know it.*
PSALM 139:14

The next time you pick up your little baby or grandbaby, look into the face of that marvelously made child and say, "[You are] fearfully and wonderfully made" (Psalm 139:14 KJV). And it wouldn't hurt to repeat that statement throughout her childhood. Children need to know how valuable they are in God's sight—and ours. Nothing gives them greater security than a strong sense of self-esteem.

Hear this well, busy parents—especially you who tend toward impatience, who are always on the run. . . . Your children have been put together in an altogether unique fashion, like no one else on earth. . . . They need you to help convince them they are unique persons, each one different, each one his or her own person. Children arrive in our arms longing to be known, longing to accept themselves as they are, to be who they are. So when they wade into the swift current of their times, they will be able to stand firm, and won't depend on peer pressure to give them their standard.

Growing Wise in Family Life

Who in your life needs to be reminded that they are fearfully and wonderfully made? How can you encourage them today?

_____

_____

49

THE OBJECT OF GOD'S CONCERN

I wait quietly before God, for my victory comes from him.
PSALM 62:1

I've had times when I've found myself wondering about the things I've believed and preached for years. What happened? Had God died? No. My vision just got a little blurry. My circumstances caused my thinking to get a little foggy. I looked up, and I couldn't see Him as clearly.

That's what happened to John Bunyan back in the seventeenth century in England. He preached against the godlessness of his day, and the authorities shoved him into prison. . . . But because Bunyan firmly believed God was still alive and working, he turned that prison into a place of praise, service, and creativity as he began to write *The Pilgrim's Progress,* the most famous allegory in the history of the English language.

When we hit a tough spot, our tendency is to feel abandoned. . . . In fact, just the opposite is true, for at that moment, we are more than ever the object of God's concern.

Elijah: A Man of Heroism & Humility

Can you think of a time when you thought you were struggling alone but, looking back, you see that God was always near and working on your behalf?

_____

_____

TAKE LIFE AS IT COMES

Plant your seed in the morning and keep busy all afternoon, for you don't know if profit will come from one activity or another—or maybe both.

ECCLESIASTES 11:6

The only way we can come to terms with reality is by trusting God, *regardless*. No ifs, ands, or buts. If I am a farmer and God allows a flood to come and wash away my crops, or if God chooses to give me the beautiful season rains and a bumper crop, I trust Him and I give Him praise. If I am in industry or some profession and someone throws me a curve and God allows my whole world to be reversed, I trust Him and I give Him praise. I take life as it occurs. I don't waste time in the pit of doubt. Nor do I worry over crop failures and strikeouts.

We can't wait for conditions to be perfect. Nor can we wait for things to be free of all risks—absolutely free, absolutely safe. Instead of protecting ourselves, we have to release ourselves. Instead of hoarding, we are to give and invest. Instead of drifting, we are to pursue life. Instead of doubting, we are to courageously trust.

Living on the Ragged Edge

Are you prone to praise in seasons of prosperity and to doubt in days of trouble? Ask the Lord to give you a steadfast heart.

_____

_____

GOD'S WAY IS RIGHT

Trust in the LORD always, for the LORD GOD is the eternal Rock.
ISAIAH 26:4

God's way is always right. It doesn't always make sense—in fact, it is often mysterious. It can seldom be explained. It isn't always pleasurable and fun. But I have lived long enough to realize that His way is always right. . . .

I believe that not until we embrace God's sovereignty will we have the ability to reason our way through life. Until then we will be *too* important in the plan. Man's opinion will be *too* significant to us. And we will churn and wrestle and struggle our way through this Christian life, trying too hard to please people rather than living it relieved and relaxed in His plan.

The Mystery of God's Will

Would you describe your day-to-day existence as relieved and relaxed? In what areas do you need to remember that God's way is always right?

_____

_____

_____

_____

_____

GOD KNOWS OUR LIMITS

But you, O Lord, are a God of compassion and mercy, slow to get angry and filled with unfailing love and faithfulness.

PSALM 86:15

Our Lord understands our limits. He realizes our struggles. He knows how much pressure we can take. He knows what measures of grace and mercy and strength we'll require. He knows how we're put together.

Frankly, His expectations are not nearly as unrealistic as ours. When we don't live up to the agenda we have set, we feel like He is going to dump a truckload of judgment on us. But that will not happen. So why do we fear it could?

Hope Again

Do you feel inadequate, overwhelmed, or ill-equipped? What unrealistic expectations have you placed on yourself?

_____

_____

_____

_____

_____

UNITY AND HUMILITY

How wonderful and pleasant it is when brothers live together in harmony!
PSALM 133:1

Do you realize how closely unity and humility are tied together? One breeds the other; neither can exist without the other. They're like Siamese twins, perpetually connected. Personally, I have seen numerous occasions when pride won out (even though it was never called that) and harmony faded away.... And I mean fast.

Contrary to the stuff you might read today, the words *fight* and *quarrel* are not apt descriptions of the way to get ahead. They won't ultimately glorify God. Friends are made *not* fighting and by *refusing* to quarrel.

Commit yourself to freeing others so they can grow and discover on their own. For a change, as much as is possible, walk away from an argument rather than inviting one. Become more of a peacemaker.

Dropping Your Guard

Is there currently conflict in some area of your life? What steps can you take to pursue humility and unity?

_____

_____

_____

_____

FROM GOD'S VANTAGE POINT

You know when I sit down or stand up. You know
my thoughts even when I'm far away.
PSALM 139:2

For Christmas one year we bought our children what was called "Ant City." This consisted of clear plastic walls on either side, filled with sand and ants. From our vantage point outside and above, we could see what these busy little creatures were doing underground. We watched as they tunneled their way around, leaving a maze of trails.

In a similar fashion, God scrutinizes our paths. From where we are, tunneling along, all we see is the sand immediately ahead, behind, and beside us. But from His vantage point, He can see exactly where we've been and precisely where we're going. He is "acquainted with all my ways" (Psalm 139:3 NASB).

The Mystery of God's Will

Do you feel like no one understands what you're going through? How does knowing that God is aware of every struggle and every success change your attitude?

_____

_____

_____

_____

CONFIDENT CONTENTMENT

Teach me to do your will, for you are my God. May your
gracious Spirit lead me forward on a firm footing.
PSALM 143:10

When Christ becomes our central focus—our reason for existence—contentment replaces our anxiety as well as our fears and insecurities. This cannot help but impact three of the most prevalent joy stealers in all of life.

1. *He broadens the dimensions of our circumstances.* This gives us new confidence.
2. *He delivers us from preoccupation with others.* This causes our contentment level to rise.
3. *He calms our fears regarding ourselves and our future.* This provides a burst of fresh hope on a daily basis.

Laugh Again

Are you experiencing the fullness of joy available to you as a believer in Christ? If not, in what areas of life have you taken your focus off of Him?

_____

_____

_____

Helping the World to See God

"In the same way, let your good deeds shine out for all to see,
so that everyone will praise your heavenly Father."

MATTHEW 5:16

The world will see "your good deeds," Jesus said. Like what?

They will hear your politeness.

They will detect your smile.

They will notice that you stop to thank them.

They will hear you apologize when you are wrong.

They will see you help them when they are struggling.

They will notice that you are the one who stopped along the road and gave them a hand.

They will see every visible manifestation of Christ's life being normally lived out through you. They will see all that and they will "glorify your Father who is in heaven" (Matthew 5:16 NASB).

We are the ones who help the world to see God.

Simple Faith

Is your faith visible to a watching world? Are you living in a way that will cause others to glorify God?

_____

_____

ABSOLUTE SILENCE

With his love, he will calm all your fears. He will
rejoice over you with joyful songs.
ZEPHANIAH 3:17

I am more convinced than ever that there is no way you and I can move toward a deeper, intimate relationship with our God without protracted times of stillness, which includes one of the rarest of all experiences: absolute silence.

Am I sounding more like a mystical dreamer? If so, so was the psalmist who wrote those familiar words we often quote but seldom obey, "Be still, and know that I am God" (Psalm 46:10 NIV).

We are commanded to stop (literally) . . . rest, relax, let go, and make time for Him. The scene is one of stillness and quietness, listening and waiting before Him. Such foreign experiences in these busy times! Nevertheless, knowing God deeply and intimately requires such discipline. Silence is indispensable if we hope to add depth to our spiritual life.

Intimacy with the Almighty

When was the last time you were completely still and silent before God? Why not try it today?

_____

_____

_____

FAITH OR PRESUMPTION?

We stopped relying on ourselves and learned to rely only on God. . . . We have placed our confidence in him, and he will continue to rescue us.

2 CORINTHIANS 1:9–10

The old motto of soldiers during the Revolutionary War applies to many areas of life: "Trust in God, but keep your powder dry!" In other words, place your life in the Savior's hands, but stay at the ready. Do all that you can to prepare yourself for battle, understanding that the ultimate outcome rests with the Lord God.

To walk by faith does not mean to stop *thinking*. To trust God does not imply becoming slovenly or lazy or apathetic. . . . You and I need to trust God for our finances, but that is no license to spend foolishly. You and I ought to trust God for safety in the car, but we're not wise to pass on a blind curve.

Acting foolishly or thoughtlessly, expecting God to bail you out if things go amiss, isn't faith at all. It is presumption. Wisdom says do all you can within your strength, then trust Him to do what you cannot do.

Moses: A Man of Selfless Dedication

In what circumstance have you done all that you can to trust God for the outcome? Or is there a situation in which you need to put more effort?

_____

_____

_____

THE ONE THING WE CAN CHANGE

The wise are mightier than the strong, and those with
knowledge grow stronger and stronger.
PROVERBS 24:5

This may shock you, but I believe the single most significant decision I can make on a day-to-day basis is my choice of attitude. It is more important than my past, my education, my paycheck, my successes or failures, fame or pain, what other people think of me or say about me, my circumstances, or my position. The attitude I choose keeps me going or cripples my progress. It alone fuels my fire or assaults my hope. When my attitudes are right, there's no barrier too high, no valley too deep, no dream too extreme, no challenge too great for me.

Yet we must admit that we spend more of our time concentrating and fretting over the things that can't be changed than we do giving attention to the one that we can change—our choice of attitude.

Day by Day with Charles Swindoll

How often do you find yourself worrying about things you can't control? What if you spent that same energy choosing a good attitude?

_____

_____

_____

SEEK RIGHTEOUSNESS

"Seek the Kingdom of God above all else, and live righteously,
and he will give you everything you need."
MATTHEW 6:33

Life is a lot like a coin; you can spend it any way you wish, but you can spend it only once. Choosing one thing over all the rest throughout life is a difficult thing to do. This is especially true when the choices are so many and the possibilities are so close at hand.

To be completely truthful with you, however, we aren't left with numerous possibilities. Jesus Himself gave us the top priority: "Seek first His kingdom and His righteousness" (Matthew 6:33 NASB).

If I am to seek first in my life God's kingdom and God's righteousness, then whatever else I do ought to relate to that goal: where I work, with whom I spend my time, the one I marry, or the decision to remain single. Every decision I make ought to be filtered through the Matthew 6:33 filter.

Living Above the Level of Mediocrity

What are you currently putting first in your life? What would it look like for you to put it aside and seek God's kingdom instead?

_____

_____

_____

Two Key Attitudes

Yet true godliness with contentment is itself great wealth.
1 Timothy 6:6

Contentment is something we must learn. It isn't a trait we're born with. But the question is, *how?* In 1 Timothy 6 we find a couple of very practical answers to that question:

A current perspective on eternity: "For we have brought nothing into the world, so we cannot take anything out of it, either" (v. 7 NASB).

A simple acceptance of essentials: "If we have food and covering, with these we shall be content" (v. 8 NASB).

Both attitudes work beautifully. . . . But society's plan of attack is to create dissatisfaction, to convince us that we must be in a constant pursuit of something "out there" that is sure to bring us happiness. . . . It says that contentment is impossible without striving for more.

God's Word offers the exact opposite advice: contentment is possible when we *stop* striving for more. Contentment never comes from externals. Never!

The Finishing Touch

Do you find yourself striving for more only to end up empty in the end? How can you choose to be content today with what the Lord has graciously provided?

_____

_____

AMAZING GRACE

*Put all your hope in the gracious salvation that will come
to you when Jesus Christ is revealed to the world.*
1 PETER 1:13

I magine coming to the house of a friend who has invited you over to enjoy a meal. You finish the delicious meal, and then listen to some fine music and visit for a while. Finally, you stand up and get your coat as you prepare to leave. But before you leave you reach into your pocket and say, "Now, how much do I owe you?" What an insult! You don't do that with someone who has graciously given you a meal.

Isn't it strange, though, how this world is running over with people who think there's something they must do to pay God back? Somehow they are hoping God will smile on them if they work real hard and earn His acceptance. But that's an acceptance on the basis of works. That's not the way it is with grace. . . .

God smiles on us because of His Son's death and resurrection. It's grace, my friend, amazing grace.

The Grace Awakening

Are you trying to earn God's favor or deserve His forgiveness? What if, instead, you embrace the beautiful gift of grace?

_____

_____

_____

IF ONLY . . .

For the happy heart, life is a continual feast.
PROVERBS 15:15

M any folks eat their hearts out, suffering from the contagious "If Only" disease. Its germs infect every slice of life.

If only I had more money.

If only we owned a nicer home.

If only we could have children.

If only he would ask me out.

If only I had more friends.

The list is endless. Woven through the fabric of all those words is a sigh that comes from the daily grind of discontentment. Taken far enough, it leads to the dead-end street of self-pity—one of the most distasteful and inexcusable of all attitudes. Discontentment is one of those daily grinds that forces others to listen to our list of woes. But they don't for long! Discontented souls soon become lonely souls.

Living Beyond the Daily Grind

What tends to stir up discontent in your heart? How can you begin replacing those things with things that encourage gratitude instead?

_____

_____

ONE DAY AT A TIME

Pride leads to disgrace, but with humility comes wisdom.
PROVERBS 11:2

People who refuse to get bogged down in and anchored to the past are those who pursue the objectives of the future. People who do this are seldom petty. They are too involved in getting a job done to be occupied with yesterday's hurts and concerns.

I know human nature well enough to realize that some people excuse their bitterness over past hurts by thinking, *It's too late to change. I've been injured, and the wrong done against me is too great for me ever to forget it.*

But when God holds out hope, when God makes promises, then God says, "It can be done." With each new dawn there is delivered to your door a fresh, new package called "today." God has designed us in such a way that we can handle only one package at a time. . . . And all the grace we need will be supplied by Him as we live out that day.

Improving Your Serve

Do you find yourself holding on to the hurts of yesterday? What if you let those things go and embrace the hope of today?

_____

_____

_____

65

HOPE IS MORE THAN DREAMING

The way of the LORD is a stronghold to those with
integrity. . . . The godly will never be disturbed.
PROVERBS 10:29–30

We toss around words like *faith* and *love* all the time. And most of us can describe both with minimal difficulty. But *hope?* What in the world is it? And is it really *that* essential?

Merriam-Webster defines *hope* as "to desire with expectation of obtainment or fulfillment." To hope is to anticipate. It is more than dreaming, however. It is possessing within ourselves an expectation that someday there will be the fulfillment of that desire. It will become a reality. Hope always looks to the future; it's always on tiptoes. It keeps us going. It makes a dismal today bearable because it promises a brighter tomorrow. Without hope, something inside all of us dies.

We can live several weeks without food, days without water, and only minutes without oxygen, but without hope—forget it.

Dropping Your Guard

When have you experienced the soul-strengthening power of hope in your life? How can you remind yourself of that hope daily?

_____

_____

_____

MARCH

PERFECT TRUST

The LORD is a shelter for the oppressed, a refuge in times of trouble.
PSALM 9:9

When the Philistines seized David in Gath he said, "When I am afraid, I will put my trust in You" (Psalm 56:3 NASB). When he fled from Saul into a cave, he cried out to God, "My soul takes refuge in You; and in the shadow of Your wings I will take refuge until destruction passes by" (Psalm 57:1 NASB).

Many, many years ago, Felix of Nola was escaping his enemies, and he, too, took temporary refuge in a cave. He had scarcely entered the opening of the cave before a spider began to weave its web across the small opening. With remarkable speed, the insect completely sealed off the mouth of the cave with an intricate web, giving the appearance that the cave had not been entered for many weeks. As Felix's pursuers passed by, they saw the web and didn't even bother to look inside. Later, as the godly fugitive stepped out into the sunlight, he uttered these insightful words: "Where God is, a spider's web is a wall; where He is not, a wall is but a spider's web."

Perfect Trust

Do you find yourself in a fearful situation? Take a moment to remind yourself that God knows how to rescue the godly.

_____

_____

THE GREAT GIFT OF FIDELITY

The trustworthy person will get a rich reward.
PROVERBS 28:20

We are living in an era that attempts to stretch grace to heretical extremes. I see it and hear it virtually every week of my life. So allow me to say this very straight: The greatest gift you can give to your marriage partner is your purity, your fidelity. The greatest character trait you can provide your spouse and your family is moral and ethical self-control. Stand firm, my friend. Refuse to yield [to temptation].

Deceptive baits are set out about us each day, and they don't all come from individuals. Some of them come from a cable television channel or the internet or a magazine or peer pressure at school or colleagues at work. . . . You'll feel like a prude, the only one around who's not yielding. Don't be deceived by the persuasion no matter how beautiful and appealing the words may sound. It is a lie. Remember, it is all a lie.

Joseph: A Man of Integrity and Forgiveness

Are there things in your life that do not promote purity or inspire righteousness? How can you begin eliminating those things today?

_____

_____

_____

GOD IS THERE, EVERY HOUR

"Don't be afraid, for I am with you. Don't be discouraged, for I am your God."
ISAIAH 41:10

Back in World War II a scribble of comic graffiti began appearing on walls everywhere, proclaiming, "Kilroy was here!" This declaration was found on walls in Germany. It was found on buildings in Tokyo. It was found on big boulders in America. Kilroy was *everywhere,* it seemed.

God is not like Kilroy. He does not write His name on the walls and rocks of life, but He is there—every day, every hour, every tick of the clock! To borrow the now-classic words of the late Francis Schaeffer, "He is there and He is not silent." Never doubt the presence of God.

He is there with you on your own personal pilgrimage . . . His unsearchable mind working in concert with His unfathomable will, carrying things out under His sovereign control.

Esther: A Woman of Strength and Dignity

Have you ever wondered if God was present and listening? How does it encourage you to know that He is with you every step of the way?

_____

_____

_____

_____

A PRESENT HELP

The LORD of Heaven's Armies is here among us; the God of Israel is our fortress.
PSALM 46:7

We deny it. We fake it. We mask it. We try to ignore it. But the truth stubbornly persists—we are *weak* creatures! Being sinful, we fail. Being prone to sickness, we hurt. Being mortal, we ultimately die. Pressure wears on us. Anxiety gives us ulcers. People intimidate us. Criticism offends us. Disease scares us. Death haunts us. . . .

How can we continue to grow in this bag of bones, covered with weaknesses too numerous to mention? We need a big dose of Psalm 46:1: "God is our refuge and strength, a very ready help in trouble" (NASB). What hope for those struggling through the grind of personal weaknesses!

Living Beyond the Daily Grind

Do you attempt to deny your weaknesses? Or, perhaps, live in shame because of them? What if, instead, you allowed God to be your strength?

_____

_____

_____

_____

_____

GOD IS IN CHARGE

Instead, I have calmed and quieted myself, like a weaned child who no longer cries for its mother's milk. Yes, like a weaned child is my soul within me.
PSALM 131:2

When it comes to irritations, I've found that it helps if I remember that I am not in charge of my day. . . . God is. And while I'm sure He wants me to use my time wisely, He is more concerned with the development of my character and the cultivation of the qualities that make me Christlike within. One of His preferred methods of training is through adjustments to irritations.

A perfect illustration? The oyster and its pearl.

Irritation occurs when the shell of the oyster is invaded by an alien substance like a grain of sand. When that happens, all the resources within the tiny, sensitive oyster rush to the irritated spot and begin to release healing fluids that otherwise would have remained dormant. By and by the irritant is covered—by a pearl. Had there been no irritating interruption, there could have been no pearl.

No wonder our heavenly home has pearly gates to welcome the wounded and bruised who have responded correctly to the sting of irritations.

The Finishing Touch

How do you respond to interruptions and irritations? What if those things are producing pearls in your life?

_____

_____

KEEP TO THE QUEST

*Get wisdom; develop good judgment. Don't forget
my words or turn away from them.*

PROVERBS 4:5

All of us are surrounded by and benefit from the results of someone's quest. Let me name a few:

Above my head is a bright electric light. Thanks, Tom.

On my nose are eyeglasses that enable me to focus. Thanks, Ben.

In my driveway is a car ready to take me wherever I choose to steer it. Thanks, Henry.

Across my shelves are books full of interesting and carefully researched pages. Thanks, authors.

My list could go on and on. So could yours.

Because some cared enough to dream, to pursue, to follow through and complete their quest, our lives are more comfortable, more stable.

That's enough to spur me on. How about you?

Day by Day with Charles Swindoll

How have you benefited from someone else's faithfulness to their quest? Who is going to benefit from your faithfulness?

_____

_____

_____

BIG-PICTURE PERSPECTIVE

You are my refuge and my shield; your word is my source of hope.
PSALM 119:114

One of the greatest benefits to be gleaned from the Bible is perspective. When we get discouraged, we temporarily lose our perspective. Little things become mammoth. A slight irritation, such as a pebble in a shoe, seems huge. Motivation is drained away and, worst of all, hope departs.

God's Word is tailor-made for gray-slush days. It sends a beam of light through the fog. It signals safety when we fear we'll never make it through. Such big-picture perspective gives us a hope transplant, and within a brief period of time, we have escaped the bleak and boring and we're back to soaring.

We can actually stand firm through discouraging times but only if we apply God's instructions.

Living Above the Level of Mediocrity

How do you keep a proper perspective? Are you spending time daily in God's Word so you can remain steadfast?

_____

_____

_____

_____

_____

GLORIFY GOD TO THE MAXIMUM

I will thank you, LORD, among all the people. I will
sing your praises among the nations.
PSALM 108:3

By making us in His image, God gave us capacities not given to other forms of life. Ideally, He made us to know Him, to love Him, and to obey Him. He did not put rings in our noses that He might pull us around like oxen.

No, He gave us freedom to make choices. By His grace we are equipped to understand His plan because we have a mind with which we can know Him. We are also free to love and adore Him because we have emotions. He takes pleasure in our affection and devotion. We can obey His instructions, but we are not pawns on a global chessboard. It is in the voluntary spontaneity of our response that He finds divine pleasure. When His people freely respond in worship and praise, obedience and adoration, God is glorified to the maximum.

Laugh Again

When did you last stop to praise God for all He has done in your life? Perhaps you could set aside time today to do just that?

_____

_____

_____

_____

WE WEEP AND PRAY, GROW AND LEARN

The LORD directs our steps, so why try to understand everything along the way?
PROVERBS 20:24

Tests are never wasted. God never says, "Oops, made a mistake on that one. I shouldn't have given you that. I meant that for Frank. Sorry, Bob." It's as if the Lord has our name on specific trials. They are specifically designed for us, arranged with our weaknesses and our immaturity in mind. He bears down and doesn't let up. And we groan and we hurt and we weep and we pray and we grow and we learn. Through it all we learn to depend upon His Word.

The common response to trials is resistance, if not outright resentment. How much better that we open the doors of our hearts and welcome the God-ordained trials as honored guests for the good they do in our lives.

Hope Again

What is your initial response to trials in your life? What are some lessons you have learned through past trials?

_____

_____

_____

_____

UNDERSTANDING AND OBEDIENCE

The Sovereign LORD *has spoken to me, and I have listened. I have not rebelled or turned away.*
ISAIAH 50:5

O ur greatest struggle is not in the realm of understanding the will of God; it's in the realm of *obeying* the God whose will it is. To be painfully honest, when you and I look back at our lives, we do not find ourselves puzzled and mystified about God's will nearly as much as we find ourselves stubborn and resistant to the One directing our steps. Our problem isn't that we don't know; our problem is that we *do* know but aren't willing to follow through.

That's the basic struggle of the Christian life. The clear truth of God is set before us time and time again. It's available to us; we read it; we hear it explained from the pulpit, in a Christian book, or on a Christian radio program; and we sense the Holy Spirit whispering, *Yes, this means you.* We understand Him clearly, but we resist. When the chips are down, our tendency is to say, "I've got it planned another way."

Moses: A Man of Selfless Dedication

In what areas do you find yourself rebelling against God's will for your life? Ask Him to give you a humble and teachable spirit.

_____

_____

LIFE IN LIVING COLOR

Truly, I love your commands more than gold, even the finest gold. Each of your commandments is right. That is why I hate every false way.
PSALM 119:127–128

The thing I have always appreciated about the Bible is that when great truth is given, God frequently incarnates that truth in lives with whom we can identify. He doesn't stop at theory as He teaches us about the abstract importance of faith. He mentions Abraham as a model who "staggered not at the promise of God through unbelief" (Romans 4:20 KJV).

He doesn't just talk about standing alone and being people of character and resiliency—He gives us Elijah. He shows us the prophets because we have much greater difficulty identifying with abstract truth. We can, however, identify with people.

God doesn't just say, "You ought to forgive." He gives us Joseph, who forgave his brothers for their mistreatment of him. God paints His heroes "warts and all." Since there are scars and a dark side to every life, we're not shielded from the Jonahs and the Samsons, from the pride of the King Sauls or the adultery of the King Davids. We see it in raw, living color.

Living on the Ragged Edge

How does it encourage or inspire you to know that the Bible is filled with real people with real stories and struggles?

_____

_____

A SWEET, WINSOME MELODY

Fix your thoughts on what is true, and honorable, and right, and pure, and lovely, and admirable. Think about things that are excellent and worthy of praise.

L et me urge you to take charge of your mind and emotions today. Let your mind feast on nutritious food for a change. Refuse to grumble and criticize! Let your life yield a sweet, winsome melody that this old world needs so desperately. Fix your attention on these six specifics in life:

Not unreal, far-fetched dreams, but things that are true . . .

Not cheap, flippant, superficial stuff, but things that are honorable . . .

Not things that are wrong and unjust, but that which is right . . .

Not thoughts that are carnal, smutty, and obscene, but that which is pure . . .

Not things that prompt arguments and defense in others, but those that are agreeable . . .

Not slander, gossip, and put-downs, but information of good report, the kind that builds up and causes grace to flow.

Strengthening Your Grip

What are your thoughts fixed on today? Are you giving your attention to things that produce a positive attitude within you?

_____

_____

_____

ENDURING FAITH

So let it grow, for when your endurance is fully developed,
you will be perfect and complete, needing nothing.
JAMES 1:4

We're very fickle in our faith, aren't we? We are inconsistent, ambivalent. We sing *"My faith looks up to Thee"*... until the medicine stops working, until the lights go out, until the bill comes due, and we don't have what it takes to pay it. Until our grades slip or our career takes a turn or we lose a mate.

How do we learn consistent faith? We learn it one day at a time. We learn it through *endurance*. James writes: "Consider it all joy, my brothers and sisters, when you encounter various trials, knowing that the testing of your faith produces endurance" (James 1:2–3 NASB). He's not talking about a will-o'-the-wisp faith that starts out on the 100-meter sprint and, quicker than you can think, is over. Anybody can handle that kind of faith. Anybody can take ten, fifteen, or twenty minutes of a test. But ten days or fifteen days, or a year, or two or three? Well, that's another matter. That's the enduring faith James is talking about.

Perfect Trust

Who do you know who lives a life of enduring faith? What practices do they have in place that produce such endurance?

_____

_____

A PROPER PERSPECTIVE

"So you cannot become my disciple without giving up everything you own."
LUKE 14:33

J esus' words are neither complicated nor vague. He simply says, "If you are going to call yourself one of My disciples, you must release your grip on materialism." To keep all this in proper perspective, think of it this way. He is not saying that we cannot possess anything, but things must not be allowed to possess us. To use His words, we must "give up" our possessions.

Corrie ten Boom, that saintly lady who endured such brutality from the Nazis in Ravensbruck during World War II, once said that she had learned to hold everything loosely in her hand. She said she discovered, in her years of walking with Him, that when she grasped things tightly, it would hurt when the Lord would have to pry her fingers loose. Disciples hold all "things" loosely.

Do you? Can you think of *anything* that has a taproot to your heart? Let go! Give it up to Him! Yes, it may be painful . . . but how essential!

Strengthening Your Grip

Give your heart an honest examination. Is there anything that you cling to tighter than Christ?

_____

_____

_____

CLAIM GOD'S GRACE

God saved you by his grace when you believed. And you
can't take credit for this; it is a gift from God.
EPHESIANS 2:8

While most people in the world are busy building towers with highest hopes of making a name and gaining fame, God's truth sets the record straight. On the basis of God's Book, His Holy Word, it is my plea that we simply admit our need and claim God's grace. Instead of striving for a man-made ticket to heaven based on high achievement and hard work (for which *we* get all the credit), I suggest we openly declare our own spiritual bankruptcy and accept God's free gift of grace. "Why?" you ask. "Why not emphasize how much I do for God instead of what He does for me?" Because that is heresy, plain and simple. How? By exalting my own effort and striving for my own accomplishments, I insult His grace and steal credit that belongs to Him only.

The Grace Awakening

Who gets the glory for the successes in your life? Have you been guilty of not giving credit where credit is due?

_____

_____

_____

_____

THE RIDDLES OF LIFE

His Spirit made the heavens beautiful, and his power pierced the gliding
serpent. . . . Who, then, can comprehend the thunder of his power?
JOB 26:13–14

There are numerous riddles in life that remain wrapped in mystery and shrouded inside an enigma. The sea, for example, is an unexplainable phenomenon. Who can fathom its tide affected strangely by the moon?

We manage to continue on, though brilliant scientists have been trying to solve and/or explain life's mysteries for years. . . . But when God leaves us with a mystery that isn't solved in a week or two, most of us go through desperate struggles believing that He is good or fair. I mean, after all, if we're going to trust a good God, He should do only good things, right? No fair doing mysterious stuff!

The Bible that I read simply doesn't present that as the way life is. Yet the world I live in seems to expect that. And that's certainly the cynic's line: "You mean to tell me you are going to trust a God who treats you like that?" When will we ever learn that cynics have no capacity to understand the profound and unfathomable ways of God?

Living on the Ragged Edge

Do you become frustrated when you can't figure out the ways of God? Are there current circumstances where you simply need to trust Him?

_____

_____

SERVING IS ESSENTIAL

Use your freedom to serve one another in love.
GALATIANS 5:13

Our world has become a large, impersonal, busy institution. We are alienated from each other. Although crowded, we are lonely. Distant. Pushed together but uninvolved. No longer do most neighbors visit across the backyard fence. The well-manicured front lawn is the modern moat that keeps barbarians at bay. Hoarding and flaunting have replaced sharing and caring. It's like we are occupying common space but have no common interests, as if we're on an elevator with rules like: "No talking, smiling, or eye contact allowed without written consent of the management."

Painful though it may be for us to admit it, we're losing touch with one another. The motivation to help, to encourage, yes, to serve our fellow man is waning. . . . And yet, it is these things that form the essentials of a happy and fulfilled life.

Improving Your Serve

What can you do today to make more meaningful connections with the people around you? How can you love and serve in tangible ways?

_____

_____

_____

GOD IS AWESOME!

Be exalted, O God, above the highest heavens. May
your glory shine over all the earth.
PSALM 108:5

When was the last time you took a glance at a mountain? You don't glance at pictures of Mount Everest and say, "Hmm, nice hill. Maybe a little taller than some mountains." You don't witness the glaciers in Alaska and say, "Oh, yeah, that's a pretty nice glacier." You stand in silent awe.

I remember when my marine battalion flew over Japan's Mount Fuji. Not one man on our plane, when they looked out and saw Fuji, said, "Sure, sure, that's nice." No, indeed! I mean, it was *click, click, click....* It was picture-taking time! *This* was picturesque, awesome Fuji!

Who made Fuji? God! And like that mountain, the rest of His creation is equally awesome. Consider the stars in space, for example. If we were to study for a lifetime, we still could not fathom them. When God does it, it makes us stand back in respect. It puts all human achievements on the lowest level.

Living on the Ragged Edge

What amazes you the most about creation: rainbows, sunsets, birds in flight? How about taking time today simply to be in awe of God's masterpiece?

_____

_____

WORRY IS DISTRACTING

Don't worry about anything; instead, pray about everything. Tell
God what you need, and thank him for all he has done.
PHILIPPIANS 4:6

A nxious. Intriguing word. It literally means "to be divided" or "distracted." We find a perfect illustration of this in the story of Mary and Martha recorded in Luke 10:38–42. Taking a minute to look into their little abode, we find that Martha is distracted, *anxious*. Jesus is sitting down talking, and Mary is sitting at His feet, enjoying His presence . . . and His teachings. But not Martha. She is busy back in the kitchen getting everything ready for a big meal. She is making everything match, everything fit, everything come out of the oven at just the right time.

But Jesus wanted her to come and sit down beside her sister and listen. It wasn't that He didn't appreciate her efforts. He just wanted her to serve a simple dish so they could make the most of their time together. . . . Her anxiety was distracting her from more important things. Worry always does that.

Perfect Trust

Worry is all-consuming. What pleasant thoughts, words of praise, or acts of worship could take its place in your life?

_____

_____

_____

No Mass-Produced Saints

Acknowledge that the LORD is God! He made us, and we are his. We are his people, the sheep of his pasture.

PSALM 100:3

We live today in a microwave culture. If it takes longer than five minutes to fix lunch, that's long! In earlier days, you even had to wait for a TV set to warm up. Can you imagine? And you couldn't push a single button on your phone to call a number; you had to *dial* it . . . with your finger, for pity's sake. Talk about the Stone Age! I remember driving by a vacant lot some time ago, then going by the same corner several weeks later. Where there had been nothing but grass and weeds, empty beer cans, and trash just days before, there was now a huge warehouse, assembled from prefab sections, ready to receive goods.

That's the way life is today. Fast. Compressed. Condensed. Slam-bang-it's-done. Not so in God's wilderness schooling. When it comes to walking with God, there is no such thing as instant maturity. God doesn't mass-produce His saints. He hand-carves each one, and it always takes longer than we expected.

Moses: A Man of Selfless Dedication

Are you sometimes impatient with the way God operates? What if, instead, you took a deep breath and embraced the slower-paced life of faith?

_____

_____

_____

GOD IN OUR CONVERSATION

*Talk about them when you are at home and when you are on the
road, when you are going to bed and when you are getting up.*
DEUTERONOMY 6:7

We are to talk of spiritual things in our homes just as we would talk about anything else. You talk together about how the Dodgers played last night. No big deal; you just talk about that. You talk about what you're going to do next week. You don't lecture on it. You don't make a big announcement; you simply talk about it. . . . You may talk about what you plan to watch on television that evening. You don't hold classes on it; you merely talk about it. There is an easygoing, natural flow of conversation.

That is what will make your Christianity authentic. It isn't a Sunday life-style! It's a Monday, Tuesday, Wednesday, Thursday, Friday, Saturday, and Sunday cycle-of-living lifestyle. So much so that Christ fits naturally into the regular conversation of the home.

Growing Wise in Family Life

How often do matters of faith come up in general conversation in your home? Is Christ a common topic of discussion?

_____

_____

_____

CONSIDERING QUITTING?

"Come to me, all of you who are weary and carry heavy burdens, and I will give you rest. . . . For my yoke is easy to bear, and the burden I give you is light."
MATTHEW 11:28, 30

E very achievement worth remembering is stained with the blood of diligence and scarred by the wounds of disappointment. To quit, to run, to escape, to hide—none of these options solve anything. They only postpone the acceptance of, and reckoning with, reality.

Churchill put it well: "Wars are not won by evacuations."

Giving thought to giving up?

Considering the possibility of quitting?

Don't! The only time the Lord ever used the word "easy" was when He referred to a yoke.

Day by Day with Charles Swindoll

Have you ever quit something only to regret it later? What examples do you see in God's Word of saints who persevered?

_____

_____

_____

_____

STAND TALL, STAND FIRM

Summon your might, O God.
PSALM 68:28

Today there are those who stand alone in the gap, those who still strive to shake us awake. A handful of brave students at Columbine High School come immediately to mind. Loaded guns and the threat of death couldn't silence them. I think of them as modern-day prophets, whom God used to deliver a life-changing message. Men and women of courage, ready to stand and deliver. Authentic heroes.

Our Lord is still searching for people who will make a difference. Christians dare not be mediocre. We dare not dissolve into the background or blend into the neutral scenery of this world.

In our culture—our schools, our offices and factories, our lunchrooms and boardrooms, our halls of ivy and our halls of justice—we need men and women of God, young people of God. We need respected professionals, athletes, home-makers, teachers, public figures, and private citizens who will promote the things of God, who will stand alone—stand tall, stand firm, stand strong!

Elijah: A Man of Heroism & Humility

Who do you know who stood firm in the face of adversity? What enabled them to do so?

_____

_____

INVINCIBLE, IMMUTABLE, AND INFINITE

All honor and glory to God forever and ever! He is the eternal
King, the unseen one who never dies; he alone is God. Amen.

1 TIMOTHY 1:17

Whoever is sovereign must have total, clear perspective. He must see the end from the beginning. He must have no match on earth or in heaven. He must entertain no fears, no ignorance, and have no needs. He must have no limitations and always know what is best. He must never make a mistake. He must possess the ability to bring everything to a purposeful conclusion and an ultimate goal. He must be invincible, immutable, infinite, and self-sufficient. His judgments must be unsearchable and His ways unfathomable. He must be able to create rather than invent, to direct rather than wish, to control rather than hope, to guide rather than guess, to fulfill rather than dream.

Who qualifies? You guessed it . . . God, and God alone.

The Mystery of God's Will

What aspect of God's sovereign nature most amazes you? Which brings you the most comfort in your current season of life?

_____

_____

_____

_____

LET GOD DO THE EXALTING

When people's lives please the LORD, even their enemies are at peace with them.
PROVERBS 16:7

Think of David, the young musician, tending his father's sheep back on the hills of Judea many centuries ago. He was a self-taught, gifted musician. He didn't go on tour, trying to make a name for himself. Instead, he sang to the sheep. He had no idea that someday his lyrics would find their way into the psalter or would be the very songs that have inspired and comforted millions of people through long and dark nights.

David didn't seek success; he simply humbled himself under the mighty hand of God, staying close to the Lord and submitting himself to Him. And God exalted David to the highest position in the land.

You don't have to promote yourself. . . . God will promote you. . . . Let God do the exalting! In the meantime, sit quietly under His hand.

Hope Again

In a world of self-promotion, followings, and platforms, what steps can you take to remain faithful in the small things of faith?

_____

_____

_____

_____

A DELIBERATE TRUST

O LORD, I have come to you for protection.

Under heaven's lock and key, we are protected by the most efficient security system available—the power of God. There is no way we will be lost in the process of suffering. No disorder, no disease, not even death itself can weaken or threaten God's ultimate protection over our lives.

"God stands between you and all that menaces your hope or threatens your eternal welfare," James Moffatt wrote. "The protection here is entirely and directly the work of God."

Two words will help you cope when you run low on hope: *accept* and *trust*.

Accept the mystery of hardship, suffering, misfortune, or mistreatment. Don't try to understand it or explain it. Accept it. Then, deliberately *trust* God to protect you by His power from this very moment to the dawning of eternity.

Hope Again

Is there a hardship in your life that the Lord is calling you to accept? Is it time to stop asking, "Why?"

_____

_____

_____

_____

CARE AND CONCERN FOR OTHERS

Dress yourselves in humility as you relate to one another, for
"God opposes the proud but gives grace to the humble."
1 PETER 5:5

Humility of mind is really an attitude, isn't it? It's a preset mentality that determines ahead of time thoughts like this:

I care about those around me.

Why do I always have to be first?

I'm going to help someone else win for a change.

Today I'm going to curb my fierce competitive tendencies.

Instead of always thinking about receiving, we'll start looking for ways to give. Instead of holding grudges against those who offend us, we'll be anxious to forgive. And instead of keeping a record of what we've done or whom we've helped, we'll take delight in forgetting the deed(s) and being virtually unnoticed. Our hunger for public recognition will diminish in significance.

Improving Your Serve

In a world where every good deed seems to be publicly proclaimed, what behind-the-scenes act of love could you perform today?

_____

_____

_____

LIVING A HOLY LIFE

"You must consecrate yourselves and be holy, because I am holy."
LEVITICUS 11:44

As Christians we live a life that is different—morally excellent, ethically beautiful. It's called a holy life. And God honors that. Because it's like He is.

Many of us have sung the old hymn "Take Time to Be Holy." Those words are true. It does take time to be holy. It certainly takes time to be mature. It takes time to cultivate a walk with the Lord that begins to flow naturally, because the enemy is so much more assertive and powerful than we . . . and so creative, so full of new ideas on how to derail us and demoralize us.

We need to lock on to the power that comes from God's presence and invite Him to cleanse our thoughts, to correct our foul speech, to forgive us completely, and make us holy vessels that, like the winged seraphim, spend our days bringing glory to His holy name.

Day by Day with Charles Swindoll

Do you get frustrated with yourself for not being where you would like to be spiritually? What is just one thing you can work on today?

_____

_____

_____

NO PLACE FOR PRIDE

Better to live humbly with the poor than to share plunder with the proud.
PROVERBS 16:19

Someone who is truly unselfish is generous with their time and possessions, energy and money. As that works its way out, it is demonstrated in various ways, such as thoughtfulness and gentleness, an unpretentious spirit, and servant-hearted leadership.

When a husband is unselfish, he subjugates his own wants and desires to the needs of his wife and family.

When a mother is unselfish, she isn't irked by having to give up her agenda or plans for the sake of her children.

When an athlete is unselfish, it is the team that matters, not winning the top honors personally.

When a Christian is unselfish, others mean more than self. Pride is given no place to operate.

Laugh Again

How do you feel when someone puts their own desires aside for your benefit? What can you do to put others first today?

_____

_____

_____

GOD'S TOPSY-TURVY WAYS

How impossible it is for us to understand his decisions and his ways!
ROMANS 11:33

God's ways are topsy-turvy to the world's ways. A few examples: God exalts the humble, but the world exalts the proud. God ascribes greatness, not to masters, but to servants. God is impressed, not with noise or size or wealth, but with quiet things . . . done in secret—the inner motives, the true heart condition. God sends away the arrogant and the rich empty-handed, but He gathers to Himself the lowly, the broken, the prisoner, the prostitute, the repentant. The world honors the handsome and the gifted and the brilliant. God smiles on the crippled, the ones who can't keep up. All this makes the world nervous.

As Dietrich Bonhoeffer wrote in *The Cost of Discipleship*: "And so the disciples are strangers in the world, unwelcome guests, disturbers of the peace. No wonder the world rejects them!"

Simple Faith

Do you find yourself impressed with the things the world deems impressive? Or do you view it all with the eyes of God?

_____

_____

_____

_____

GOD SPEAKS TO THE QUIET HEART

A single day in your courts is better than a thousand anywhere else!
PSALM 84:10

If the pace and the push, the noise and the crowds are getting to you, it's time to stop the nonsense and find a place of solace to refresh your spirit. Deliberately say "no" more often. This will leave room for you to slow down, get alone, pour out your overburdened heart, and admit your desperate need for inner refreshment. The good news is God will hear and He will help. The bad news is this: if you wait for someone else to bring about a change, things will only deteriorate.

All of us can testify, God does not speak to the hurried, worried mind. It takes time alone with Him and His Word before we can expect our spiritual strength to recover.

Intimacy with the Almighty

Has your busyness become a burden? What activities do you need to remove from your agenda in order to make time for stillness in your day?

_____

_____

_____

_____

_____

APRIL

A GIANT STEP TOWARD MATURITY

*My health may fail, and my spirit may grow weak, but God
remains the strength of my heart; he is mine forever.*
PSALM 73:26

One of the hardest things for you and me to do is own up to our own failures. Whether we're talking to our spouses, our kids, our employers, or with our Lord Himself, it goes against the grain to come clean and admit our offenses. The knee-jerk response every time is to employ defense mechanisms: to deny, to excuse, to rationalize, to *reinterpret* our shortfalls.

The best and healthiest course is to 'fess up. To call failure, "failure." To name sin for what it is. To admit we were wrong, and having declared it, to learn what God may have to teach us from the experience.

Sir Winston Churchill . . . offered the best definition of success I've ever read: "Success is moving from one failure to another with no loss of enthusiasm." . . . As you begin to interpret failure correctly, you will take your first giant step toward maturity.

Moses: A Man of Selfless Dedication

What lessons in the past have you learned from failure? How have you seen spiritual growth stem from those experiences?

_____

_____

SOW GENEROUSLY, REAP GENEROUSLY

Let all that I am praise the LORD; with my whole heart, I will praise his holy name.
PSALM 103:1

Do you have eyesight? It's a gift. Do you have a good mind? It's a gift. Do you have leadership abilities that cause others to follow? A good education? These are all gifts. Has God given you a family? Has He given you sufficient clothes? . . . These are all gifts from God's hand. Reflect on His numerous gifts to you. It will increase your joy.

Then remind yourself of God's promises regarding generosity. God promises if you sow bountifully, you will reap bountifully. So give! Give abundantly! Even extravagant giving is honored by God. I've never known anyone who went bad because he or she was too generous. Remind yourself of His promises regarding generosity and start giving!

Don't be afraid of out-giving God. It is absolutely impossible to do that.

Living Above the Level of Mediocrity

How can you imitate the lavish generosity of God? What are some ways you can give abundantly and selflessly to those around you?

_____

_____

_____

SEEKING SUCCESS

Pride leads to disgrace, but with humility comes wisdom.
PROVERBS 11:2

We are a success-saturated society. The telltale signs are everywhere. Each year dozens of books and magazines, scores of audiobooks and podcasts, and hundreds of seminars offer ideas, motivations, techniques, and promises of prosperity.

Curiously, however, few ever address what it is most folks want (but seldom find) in their pursuit of success: contentment, fulfillment, satisfaction, and relief.

At the risk of sounding ultra-simplistic, I'd like to offer some counsel to those seeking success.

First, submit yourself to those who are wise.

Second, humble yourself under God's mighty hand.

Third, throw yourself on the mercy and care of God.

The Finishing Touch

What does success mean to you? Do you look to the world or the Word for your definition?

_____

_____

_____

MAGNIFICENT RELIEF

I confessed all my sins to you . . . and you forgave me! All my guilt is gone.
PSALM 32:5

Like a cool, cleansing shower on a hot, sweaty day, God's forgiveness washes away not only sins but their tormenting guilt. God goes into the depths of our inner being and provides that magnificent relief that only He can bring: peace.

If you are harboring some sin—if you are keeping hidden a few secret regions of wrong—don't expect to enjoy freedom from guilt, child of God. There is an unspoken axiom threaded through Scripture: secret sin cannot coexist with inner peace. Peace returns only when our sins are fully confessed and forsaken. Few grinds are more galling than the grind of an unforgiven conscience. It's awful! And few joys are more relieving than having our sins forgiven. It's wonderful!

Living Beyond the Daily Grind

Do you need to experience the freedom of forgiveness today? Confess your sins to the Lord and experience His peace.

_____

_____

_____

_____

WHAT TO DO WITH WORRY

"So don't worry about tomorrow, for tomorrow will bring its own worries. Today's trouble is enough for today."
MATTHEW 6:34

Here's a question worth your time: What are we to do when worry comes knocking on the doors of our minds? First, we must set our minds on Christ. "Seek first His kingdom and His righteousness, and all these things will be provided to you" (Matthew 6:33 NASB). When the temptation to worry first arrives, that's the critical moment. The tendency is to entertain it. To let it onto the front porch and allow it to sit there. But before you know it, worry has crawled in through the window and made itself at home! No, worry must be stopped. We have to decide that we are going to commit this worry to God right now and refuse to entertain it, even on the front porch of our thinking.

Perfect Trust

Do you tend to entertain worries for far too long? Why not begin turning them over to God today?

_____

_____

_____

_____

_____

MEANINGFUL MEMORIALS

*These days would be remembered and kept from generation to generation and
celebrated by every family throughout the provinces and cities of the empire.*
ESTHER 9:28

The Lincoln Memorial. The Vietnam Memorial. . . . Memorials are places
provided for us to stand and be quiet, to reflect, and to pass on to the next
generation the roots of a nation's heritage. They give the present significance
because they give the past perspective.

My fear for our present, rapid-paced lifestyle is that we have so few memorials, so few monuments, even mental monuments. Life is lived in the fast lane.
Superficial decisions. Hurry-up childhoods. . . . So little time spent stopping and
recording segments of our lives in a journal. So little emphasis on listening and
learning and honoring.

In order to have perspective, we must have monuments and memorials,
places to return to and learn from and talk about and pass on. If we don't, we
are destined to live rootless, fast-lane lives without much significance.

Esther: A Woman of Strength and Dignity

What can you do to make sure those coming after you know what the
Lord has done in your life? Are there memorials that point to Him?

_____

_____

_____

SACRED SERENDIPITY

"I will once again astound these hypocrites with amazing wonders."
ISAIAH 29:14

S eren-dip-ity—the *dip* of the *serene* into the common responsibilities of life.
Serendipity occurs when something beautiful breaks into the monotonous
and the mundane. A serendipitous life is marked by "surprisability" and spontaneity. When we lose our capacity for either, we settle into life's ruts. We expect
little and we're seldom disappointed.

Though I have walked with God for several decades, I must confess I still
find much about Him incomprehensible and mysterious. But this much I know:
He delights in surprising us. He dots our pilgrimage from earth to heaven with
amazing serendipities.

Your situation may be as hot and barren as a desert or as forlorn and meaningless as a wasteland. . . . But all I ask is that you . . . be on the lookout. God may
very well be planning a serendipity in your life.

The Finishing Touch

When have you been delightfully surprised by God? Do you live with an
expectation that He will show up in your life?

_____

_____

_____

Forever Discontented

*"Beware! Guard against every kind of greed. Life is
not measured by how much you own."*
LUKE 12:15

Let's take a brief look at greed. Practically speaking, greed is an inordinate desire for more, an excessive, unsatisfied hunger to possess. Like an untamed beast, greed grasps, claws, reaches, clutches, and clings—stubbornly refusing to surrender. The word *enough* is not in this beast's vocabulary. Akin to envy and jealousy, greed is nevertheless distinct. Envy wants to have what someone else possesses. Jealousy wants to possess what it already has. But greed is different. Greed is forever discontented and therefore insatiably craving, longing, wanting, striving for more, more, more.

That's the whole point of greed. You'll want more and more of something that really isn't good for you. And in the getting of it, you'll suffer the painful consequences. That's why Jesus warns, "Beware. Be on your guard. This thing is like a cancer—an insatiable leech that will suck the life right out of you." Enough will never be enough. Beware.

Living Above the Level of Mediocrity

Have you found yourself in the cruel grip of greed? How can you choose a life of contentment instead?

_____

_____

OUTRAGEOUS JOY

You will show me the way of life, granting me the joy of your
presence and the pleasures of living with you forever.
PSALM 16:11

I know of no greater need today than the need for joy. Unexplainable, contagious joy. Outrageous joy.

When that kind of joy comes aboard our ship of life, it brings things with it—like enthusiasm for life, determination to hang in there, and a strong desire to be of encouragement to others. Such qualities make our voyage bearable when we hit the open seas and encounter high waves of hardship that tend to demoralize and paralyze. There is nothing better than a joyful attitude when we face the challenges life throws at us.

Someone once asked Mother Teresa what the job description was for anyone who might wish to work alongside her in the grimy streets and narrow alleys of Calcutta. Without hesitation she mentioned only two things: the desire to work hard and a joyful attitude.

Laugh Again

How has a joyful attitude helped you endure painful trials? What can you do to maintain a joyful spirit?

_____

_____

THE SHELTERING TREE OF FRIENDSHIP

A friend is always loyal, and a brother is born to help in time of need.
PROVERB 17:17

The poet Samuel Coleridge once described friendship as "a sheltering tree." When you have this quality, the branches of your friendship reach out over the lives of others, giving them shelter, shade, rest, relief, and encouragement.

Friends give comfort. We find strength near them. They bear fruit that provides nourishment and encouragement. When something troublesome occurs in our life, we pick up the phone and call a friend, needing the comfort he or she provides. I think there are few things lonelier than having no friend to call. Friends also care enough about us to hold us accountable . . . but we never doubt their love or respect.

Hope Again

Who in your life is struggling and needs the shelter of your friendship? How can you reach out to them today?

_____

_____

_____

_____

_____

PRIORITIES FOR PARENTS

My child, if your heart is wise, my own heart will rejoice!
PROVERBS 23:15

L et me make three practical suggestions to you who are parents.

First, *determine your priorities.* Ask yourself how high the family rates on your list of involvement. How are your children in particular—just how serious are you regarding time with each? Have you told them or your mate?

Second, *record your observations.* If a child reveals their struggles in everyday life, those things are worth writing down. Keep a journal on each child. . . . As you write, pray for wisdom. Ask God to guide your thoughts. Please remember, each child is unique. No comparisons!

Third, *share your findings.* Children long to know themselves better. They respect your counsel and will long remember your remarks. Be candid and honest as you help them "see" who they really are.

Growing Wise in Family Life

How much time do you spend praying for and studying your children? Do you share insights with them?

_____

_____

_____

_____

THE IMPOSSIBLE IS GOD'S IDEAL

Don't be afraid. Just stand still and watch the LORD rescue you today.

EXODUS 14:13

I'd like to underline a major truth in this world of ours that I don't pretend to understand. Here it is: the best framework for the Lord God to do His most ideal work is when things are absolutely impossible and we feel totally unqualified to handle it. That's His favorite circumstance. Those are His ideal working conditions.

God does His most magnificent work when the situation seems totally impossible from a human point of view, and we feel absolutely unprepared and unable to do anything about it, *yet our eyes are on Him*. . . . That's when God rolls up His big sleeves and says, "Step back out of the way a moment, and watch Me work."

Time after time, He brings us to our absolute end and then proves Himself faithful. That, my friend, is the story of the Bible in a nutshell.

Moses: A Man of Selfless Dedication

Are you prone to panic when a situation seems hopeless? What if, instead, you prepared to be amazed by God at work?

_____

_____

_____

A BEAUTIFUL BALANCE

Whoever pursues righteousness and unfailing love
will find life, righteousness, and honor.
PROVERBS 21:21

We've been programmed to think that fatigue is next to godliness. That the more exhausted we are (and look!), the more committed we are to spiritual things, and the more we earn God's smile of approval. . . . As a result, we have become a generation of people who worship our work . . . who work at our play . . . and who play at our worship.

Hold it! Who wrote that rule? Why have we bought that philosophy? Whatever possessed someone to make such a statement? How did we ever get caught in that maddening undertow?

I challenge you to support it from the Scriptures. Start with the life (and *lifestyle*) of Jesus Christ. . . . His was a life of beautiful balance. He accomplished everything the Father sent Him to do. Everything. And He did it without ignoring those essential times of restful leisure. If that is the way *He* lived, then it makes good sense that is the way we too must learn to live.

Strengthening Your Grip

Do you struggle maintaining a balance with work and play and worship and rest? Do you allow adequate time in your schedule for each?

_____

_____

HEED GOD'S PROMPTINGS

We can make our plans, but the LORD determines our steps.

PROVERBS 16:9

Nothing wrong with planning. Nothing wrong with thinking it through. Nothing wrong with doing your charts, listing all the pros and cons, talking it over. But as you are moving along, stay sensitive to the quiet, yet all-important prompting of God through His Holy Spirit. It's easier to steer a moving car. Just get the car rolling and you can push it into the filling station to get the gas. But it's hard to get it moving from a dead stop. So you're on your way, you're making your plans, you're thinking it through. Just stay open.

As author Henry Blackaby says, "Watch to see where God is at work and join Him!" Just go there. Why do you want to be anywhere God *isn't* at work?

The Mystery of God's Will

What ideas or dreams has God placed within you? Are you planning and praying about how those things may come about?

_____

_____

_____

_____

_____

WISDOM IN THE WILDERNESS

I will teach you wisdom's ways and lead you in straight paths.
PROVERBS 4:11

The Hebrew word for *desert* is *midbaar*. It's from the word *dahbaar*, meaning "to speak." Let me draw from that root term and suggest that the desert is the place where God speaks, where He communicates some of His most important messages to us.

Your desert experience might involve caring for an ailing family member or an elderly parent over an extended time, with no help at hand and no relief in sight. Your sojourn in the dry lands might be a stubborn physical condition that keeps you confined. It could be that deep soul-ache that comes with an unfaithful spouse or a rebellious teenager.

Does God know? Does He understand? He understands very well, my friend. After all, He's the One who *put* you there. His schooling includes time in the wilderness. That's where He gets our attention.

Moses: A Man of Selfless Dedication

When have you found yourself in a wilderness with the Lord? What lessons did you learn while there?

_____

_____

_____

A WORRY OR TWO OR THREE . . .

"Can all your worries add a single moment to your life?"
LUKE 12:25

I n the depths of every person's soul, in the secret chambers where no one else knows the thoughts, we are usually able to find a worry or two or three. Even in the hearts of those who are laughing and smiling.

We worry about death—our own or that of a loved one. We worry about disobedience and sin, about feelings of guilt. We worry about daily problems—people problems, decision problems, problems related to work, home, relationships, finances, school . . . you name it, we worry about it.

One of the problems with worry is that *it keeps you from enjoying what you have.* When you worry about what you don't have, you won't be able to enjoy what you do have. That's what Jesus was talking about in Matthew 6:25: "I say to you, do not be worried about your life, as to what you will eat or what you will drink" (NASB). Worry is assuming responsibilities that you cannot handle. The truth is, they are responsibilities that God never intended for you to handle, because they are His.

Perfect Trust

Do your worries keep you up at night? Why not turn them over to the One who neither slumbers nor sleeps?

_____

_____

GOD'S TRUTH INCARNATED

For their command is a lamp and their instruction a light;
their corrective discipline is the way to life.
PROVERBS 6:23

The tyranny of the urgent will always out-shout the essential nature of the important . . . if we let it. We have to determine not to let that happen. The secret is establishing personal priorities. I have suggested four:

Set a firm foundation—be *biblical*.

Apply the truth of the Scriptures—be *authentic*.

Develop a compassionate attitude—be *gracious*.

Stay current, always up to date—be *relevant*.

As we begin to do this, Christianity becomes something that is absorbed, not just worn. It is more than believed; it is incarnated.

And if there is anything that will catch the attention of preoccupied people fighting the fires of the urgent, it is God's truth incarnated. It happened in the first century, and it can happen in the twenty-first. Even in an aimless world like ours.

Strengthening Your Grip

Are you more likely to be preoccupied with the urgent or the important? How can you begin focusing on what truly matters?

_____

_____

BEAUTIFUL IN GOD'S TIME

Yet God has made everything beautiful for its own time.
ECCLESIASTES 3:11

Among Christians a favorite verse of Scripture is Romans 8:28: "And we know that God causes all things to work together for good to those who love God, to those who are called according to His purpose" (NASB). The key part of the verse is "work together." That verse does not say "all things are good"—just as Solomon's comment does not say "everything is beautiful." It says all things are good as they work together for His purpose.

Ecclesiastes 3:11 says, "He has made everything beautiful *in its time*" (NKJV). And I've got news for those who struggle with God's timing. You may not live to see God's time completely fulfilled. You may live to a ripe old age, carry out your reason for existence, and die before the full program of God has reached its ultimate and completed purpose. But His promise stands—He will make everything beautiful in its time.

Living on the Ragged Edge

Do you believe that God will make all things beautiful in time? How does that understanding help you remain faithful today?

_____

_____

_____

WISDOM JUST IN TIME

"Don't worry about how to respond or what to say. God
will give you the right words at the right time."
MATTHEW 10:19

D o you know what I've discovered about the Lord? He doesn't give wisdom on credit. He doesn't advance you a bundle of insight. . . . Do you know when He gives us words and wisdom and insight? *Right when we need them.* At the very instant they are required.

If you're a parent, you may have experienced this phenomenon. You find yourself in a situation you never anticipated and couldn't prepare for. Suddenly, you're at one of the critical junctures of life where you're the mom or dad, and your child is looking into your eyes, depending on you for a right answer. Not always, but often, you are given the words you need. Later you realize that they were words beyond your own wisdom. At that quiet moment, you breathe a little prayer of thanks. "Praise You, Lord. That's exactly what needed to be said."

Moses: A Man of Selfless Dedication

Can you think of a time when God gave you the right words for the right time? Or when someone somehow had the right words to minister to you?

_____

_____

_____

THE SOVEREIGN POTTER

And yet, O LORD, you are our Father. We are the clay, and you are the potter.
ISAIAH 64:8

By now in our Christian walk we hardly need the reminder that life is not a cloud-nine utopia. It is a terribly unrealistic view to think that Christ helps you live happily ever after; it's downright unbiblical! Most of life is learning and growing, falling and getting back up, forgiving and forgetting, accepting and going on.

We know the sovereign Potter is working with our clay as He pleases. I've watched a few potters at work. And it's a funny thing. I have seen them suddenly mash the clay down and start over again. Each time they do this, the clay comes out looking entirely different. And with gifted potters, they can start over and over—and each time it's better and better.

He is the Potter; we are the clay. He is the One who gives the commands; we are the ones who obey. . . . He is shaping us into the image of His Son.

Day by Day with Charles Swindoll

Have you ever felt like you were being mashed down under the hand of God? What if He is doing so to build you up to look more like Jesus?

_____

_____

_____

GOD MADE ME

*You made all the delicate, inner parts of my body and knit me together
in my mother's womb. Thank you for making me so wonderfully
complex! Your workmanship is marvelous—how well I know it.*
PSALM 139:13–14

The word *formed* literally means "originated or created." God reached into my life when I was merely a tiny embryo and began to shape me within. He originated me. He began to put me together while I was still in the soft silence of my mother's womb. It was there my "inward parts" were originated by God.

The nine-month interweaving work of God included my likes and dislikes, my personality as well as my perspective on life.

As I analyze my body and see the way I have been put together, I join the psalmist in praise and gratitude to God, my Creator.

Mother Nature didn't make me. Fate did not shape me. Neither was I just a biological combination of mother and dad in a moment of sexual passion. Nor was I conceived through blind chance. You, God (and no other), made me!

Growing Wise in Family Life

Do you struggle with certain aspects of your makeup or personality? What if you saw them as part of God's marvelous craftsmanship?

_____

_____

LEAVE IT TO GOD

And this righteousness will bring peace. Yes, it will
bring quietness and confidence forever.
ISAIAH 32:17

Can't seem to get where you want to go fast enough? *Leave it to God.*
Worried about your kids? *Leave it to God.*
Living in a place you'd rather not be? *Leave it to God.*
Looks like you won't graduate with honors? *Leave it to God.*
Found a lump and you see the doctor tomorrow? *Leave it to God.*
A mid-career change seems scary? *Leave it to God.*
You did the job but someone else got the credit? *Leave it to God.*

Day by Day with Charles Swindoll

Are you overwhelmed with all the cares of this life? Do you trust God to handle each and every one of them? Leave them to Him.

_____

_____

_____

_____

_____

_____

OUR WILL OR GOD'S WILL?

"I will guide you along the best pathway for your life.
I will advise you and watch over you."
PSALM 32:8

Following the will of God requires faith and action, which in turn call for risk and release. This is where things get very personal; this is where we persevere and flesh out the will of God.

I have come to this conclusion: Doing the will of God is rarely easy and uncomplicated. Instead, it is often difficult and convoluted. Or . . . *mysterious*. Because we don't know where He is taking us, we must bend our wills to His—and most of us are not all that excited about bending. We'd much prefer resisting. That's why the Christian life is often such a struggle. I don't mean that it's a constant marathon of misery. It's just a struggle between our will and His will. Someday, when we are caught up with the Lord in glory, we will finally be all the things we have longed to be. Until then, we live in this never-ending tension of give and take, push and pull.

The Mystery of God's Will

In what area of life do you feel yourself resisting instead of bending? Do you trust God enough to give in to His perfect will?

_____

_____

_____

GRACE FOR EVERY SHADE OF SORROW

*So when your faith remains strong through many trials, it
will bring you much praise and glory and honor.*

1 PETER 1:7

Trials come in various forms. The word *various* comes from an interesting Greek term, *poikolos,* which means "variegated" or "many-colored." We also get the term "polka dot" from it. Trials come in a variety of forms and colors. They are different, just as we are different. Something that would hardly affect you might knock my feet out from under me—and vice versa. But God offers special grace to match every shade of sorrow.

This variety of trials is like different temperature settings on God's furnace. The settings are adjusted to burn off our dross, to temper us or soften us according to what meets our highest need. It is in God's refining fire that the authenticity of our faith is revealed. And the purpose of these fiery ordeals is that we may come forth as purified gold, a shining likeness of the Lord Jesus Christ Himself.

Hope Again

What fiery trials have you been through in your life? How have they made you more like Christ?

_____

_____

_____

123

TAKE IT BY FAITH

"For just as the heavens are higher than the earth, so my ways are higher than your ways and my thoughts higher than your thoughts."
ISAIAH 55:9

Despite all of our searching and all of our study of the Scriptures, we'll never be able to see everything clearly, to fully grasp and understand and answer all the questions. They are beyond our comprehension—a puzzle, a mystery.

In *Keep a Quiet Heart*, Elisabeth Elliot said, "Today is mine. Tomorrow is none of my business. If I peer anxiously into the fog of the future, I will strain my spiritual eyes so that I will not see clearly what is required of me now."

Much of what happens in life we simply have to take by faith. Answers will not be forthcoming. These are the tensions of reality, and if we get marooned on the tensions, we will not be able to travel further. That is as our heavenly Father planned it.

The Mystery of God's Will

How many of your current worries are about things that may or may not happen in the future? How much more joy would you have if you focused only on today?

_____

_____

_____

A DEAD-END ROAD

Pride goes before destruction, and haughtiness before a fall.

PROVERBS 16:18

What is it that drives us on so relentlessly? Are you ready? Take a deep breath and allow yourself to tolerate the one-word answer: pride. We work and push and strive so we can prove we are worthy . . . we are the best . . . we deserve top honors. And the hidden message: I can gain righteousness all on my own, by my own effort, ingenuity, and energy. And because I can, I must! And why is this heretical? Because ultimately this philosophy says: (1) I really don't need divine righteousness (after all, God helps those who help themselves, right?), and (2) I will find lasting joy in my own achievement. This will bring me ultimate satisfaction.

Both are dead-end roads found on Fantasy Island.

Laugh Again

Do you find yourself trying to earn God's favor? Why is the free gift of grace often hard to accept?

_____

_____

_____

_____

_____

GREAT-HEARTED SOULS

*"God blesses those who work for peace, for they
will be called the children of God."*
MATTHEW 5:9

Peacemakers release tension; they don't intensify it. Peacemakers seek solutions and find no delight in arguments. Peacemakers calm the waters; they don't trouble them. Peacemakers work hard to keep an offense from occurring. And if it has occurred, they strive for resolution. Peacemakers lower their voices rather than raise them. Peacemakers generate more light than heat. Blessed are such great-hearted souls!

Make no mistake, however; *peacemaker* is not a synonym for "appeaser." This is not peace at any price. There are limits. . . . Smiling at wrongdoing or erroneous teaching doesn't simplify life; it complicates it.

When Christ blessed the peacemakers, He was extolling the value of doing all we can to maintain harmony and support unity. His interest was in making peace where peace is an appropriate objective.

Simple Faith

Are there offenses you need to overlook or wrongs you need to forgive?
How can you begin making peace today?

_____

_____

_____

A CLUTTERED, COMPLICATED WORLD

*God created people to be virtuous, but they have each
turned to follow their own downward path.*

ECCLESIASTES 7:29

E verything around us works against reordering and simplifying our lives. Everything! Ours is a cluttered, complicated world. God did not create it that way. Depraved, restless humanity has made it that way!

Advertisements have one major goal: to make us discontented, woefully dissatisfied with who we are and what we have. Why? So we will acquire what they offer. And acquire we do! The watchword of our consumptive society is very loud and assertive—*more*! Enough is never enough.

Not only do we acquire . . . we keep, we accumulate. Furthermore, we don't simply compete . . . we are driven to win, always win. And not only do we want more, we must spend more time maintaining those things. Staying ahead of that maddening pace leaves us strained, fretful, breathless.

Surely, God is not the author of such confusion.

Intimacy with the Almighty

Would you call yourself content? Or have you fallen into the trap of always wanting more?

_____

_____

_____

PERFECT IN HIM

Yet now he has reconciled you. . . . You are holy and blameless
as you stand before him without a single fault.
COLOSSIANS 1:22

L iving as we do in a product-oriented culture, we like to package our faith too. We prefer to sell a slick, shrink-wrapped version of salvation that includes happiness and peace, happiness here and now, and heaven by and by. While there is nothing wrong with good marketing techniques or teaching principles of authentic success, there is something wrong if we neglect to mention the *process*, which must inevitably include times of defeat and failure.

What I'd like to know is who erected such a happily-ever-after standard of perfection in the first place? God knows very well we aren't able to produce perfection; that's why Jesus, the perfect Son of God, placed us in His family. That's why He gave us a position of perfect righteousness in Him, reminding us by contrast that our own daily experience will constantly fall short.

Moses: A Man of Selfless Dedication

Are you surprised when you encounter hardships and trials? What would you say to someone else who thinks salvation will bring an easy life?

_____

_____

_____

ROOT OUT REBELLION

*Blessed are those who fear to do wrong, but the
stubborn are headed for serious trouble.*

PROVERBS 28:14

In a world hell-bent on having its own way, it is terribly difficult to cultivate the right attitude toward authority. The "Question authority!" mentality is so interwoven into the fabric of our society, it seems impossible to counteract it. Realistically, about the only place we can come to terms with it is in our homes. Are you doing this? Be honest, now. Within the walls of your dwelling are you maintaining the controls? Maybe these three warnings will encourage you to stay at it . . . or start today.

Childhood. A rebellious nature is conceived in a home where parents relinquish control.

Adolescence. A rebellious spirit will be cultivated among peers who resist control. And if it isn't curbed there, it culminates at—

Adulthood. A rebellious life must be crushed by God when He regains control.

And take it from one who experienced it and deals with it week after week—nothing is more painful to endure.

Strengthening Your Grip

Have you experienced the consequences of rebellion in your life? What can you do (or have you done) to regain control?

_____

_____

MAY

A RADICAL DECISION

Don't lose sight of common sense and discernment. . . . They
keep you safe on your way, and your feet will not stumble.

PROVERBS 3:21, 23

We are like tiny islands of truth surrounded by a sea of paganism, but we launch our ships every day. We can't live or do business in this world without rubbing shoulders with those driven by the world's desires. God calls very few to be monks in a monastery. So we must make a practical decision not to be conformed while we are in the system, and at the same time, we must make a radical decision to give God the green light to transform our minds.

At the deepest level, even though the majority may not want to admit it, most people are conformists. That is why it is correctly termed a radical decision. Only a radically different mindset can equip folks like us to stand alone when we're outnumbered.

It takes courage to think alone, to resist alone, to stand alone—especially when the crowd seems so safe, so right.

Living Above the Level of Mediocrity

In what situations is it most difficult to stand firm in your faith? Where do you find the courage and confidence to resist peer pressure?

_____

_____

_____

GOD'S GRACIOUS LIBERTY

We know that our old sinful selves were crucified with
Christ so that sin might lose its power in our lives.
ROMANS 6:6

I remember one hot and humid Houston afternoon back in grade school when our teacher gave everyone permission to go barefoot after lunch. We got to pull off our socks, stick 'em in our sneakers, and wiggle our toes all we wanted to. During the afternoon recess that extra freedom added great speed to our softball game on the playground.

Isn't it strange then, now that you and I are grown and have become Christians, how reluctant we are to give ourselves permission to do . . . to think . . . to say . . . to buy and enjoy . . . or to be different and not worry about who may say what?

Even though our God has graciously granted us permission to be free, to have liberty . . . and to enjoy so much of this life, many in His family seldom give themselves permission.

The Finishing Touch

What is something you do simply because it brings you joy? And why don't you do it more often?

_____

_____

_____

LIGHT AND TRUTH

Send out your light and your truth; let them guide me.

PSALM 43:3

In this psalm David asked for two specific things: *light* and *truth*. He wanted God to give him His Word (truth) and an understanding of it (light).

Every believer in Jesus Christ must ultimately come to the place where he is going to trust God's Word completely before he can experience consistent victory. It is our single source of tangible truth. We try every other crutch—we lean on self . . . on others . . . on feelings . . . on bank accounts . . . on good works . . . on logic and reason . . . on human perspective—and we continually end up with the short straw. God has given His written Word and the promise of His light to all His children. When will we ever learn to believe it and live in it and use it and claim it? I often wonder how many of His personal promises to His people exist in His Book unclaimed and ignored.

Living Beyond the Daily Grind

Where do you turn for the truth? Consider a time when you turned to God's Word and compare it to a time when you didn't.

_____

_____

_____

_____

GOD TAKES CARE OF YOU

"Be strong and courageous! Do not be afraid or discouraged.
For the LORD your God is with you wherever you go."
JOSHUA 1:9

D id you know that worry erases the promises of God from your mind? Jesus implies this when He says, "And if God cares so wonderfully for wildflowers that are here today and thrown into the fire tomorrow, he will certainly care for you. Why do you have so little faith? So don't worry about these things, saying, 'What will we eat? What will we drink? What will we wear?'" (Matthew 6:30–31 NLT). The promise of God is that He will care for us. He will care for our needs, and that's the promise you can claim. Since He took care of our greatest need at Calvary by giving us Christ, then you can be sure He will take care of everything else He considers important for us.

Perfect Trust

What worries currently occupy space in your mind? What promises of God do you need to claim to remove those anxious thoughts?

_____

_____

_____

_____

TRIUMPHANT HOPE

The hopes of the godly result in happiness.

PROVERBS 10:28

One of the great themes of Christianity is triumphant hope. Not just hope as in a distant, vague dream, but *triumphant* hope, the kind of hope where all things end right. In the midst of the struggles and the storms and the sufferings of life, we can advance our thoughts beyond today and see relief . . . triumph . . . victory. Because, in the end, God does indeed win.

Think that through. All earthly woes, all financial pressures, all emotional trauma, all physical disabilities and handicaps, all domestic conflicts . . . all that ends. And we will be with Him who wins! And that means nothing but harmony and unity and victory and joy and praise and delight.

We'll be changed down inside. We'll have new natures. We'll have new minds. We'll have new bodies. We'll have the joy of living forever and ever in praise and adoration of our God.

Esther: A Woman of Strength and Dignity

Do you believe that God will make all things right in the end? How does that help you persevere today?

_____

_____

_____

YOUR WORK IS NOT IN VAIN

*Let's not get tired of doing what is good. At just the right time
we will reap a harvest of blessing if we don't give up.*
GALATIANS 6:9

S omeone once counted all the promises in the Bible and came up with an
amazing figure of almost 7,500. Among that large number are some specific
promises God's servants can claim today. Believe me, there are times when the
only thing that will keep you going is a promise from God that your work is not
in vain.

When we have done what was needed, but were ignored, misunderstood, or
forgotten . . . we can be sure it was not in vain.

When we did what was right, with the right motive, but received no credit,
no acknowledgment, not even a "thank you" . . . we have God's promise that
"we will reap."

The Finishing Touch

Have you ever been overlooked or unappreciated? How does it feel
knowing that your heavenly Father will reward you for your efforts?

_____

_____

_____

_____

A RARE COMMODITY

Pride ends in humiliation, while humility brings honor.
PROVERBS 29:23

Humility isn't a show we put on; in fact, if we think we're humble, we're probably not. And in our day of self-promotion, self-assertion, spotlighting "celebrities of the faith," and magnifying the flesh, this quality—so greatly valued by the Lord Jesus—is a rare commodity indeed.

A truly humble person looks for opportunities to give himself freely to others rather than hold back, to release rather than hoard, to build up rather than tear down, to serve rather than be served, to learn from others rather than clamor for the teaching stand. How blessed are those who learn this early in life.

Hope Again

What are you currently putting first in your life? What would it look like for you to put it aside and seek God's kingdom instead?

_____

_____

_____

_____

_____

_____

LET GO, RELAX

A house is built by wisdom and becomes strong through good sense.
PROVERBS 24:3

The older I get, the more I appreciate the benefits of taking time. Woodwork done slowly and meticulously by a craftsman is beautiful and able to endure the test of the elements. Art—whether musical compositions, needle-work, sculpture, or painting—requires time and attention to detail. Even the cultivation of our walk with God . . . requires a great deal of time to develop.

The psalmist realized this when he wrote, "Be still, and know that I am God" (Psalm 46:10). The Hebrew does not suggest standing around and let-ting your mind wander—not that kind of being still. Rather, it means "Let go. Relax."

If all this is true of other realms and responsibilities, it is certainly appli-cable to the home and family. Children were not created to be "jerked up" (as my mother used to put it), but to be cared for with gentleness and attention to detail. They require time . . . lots of it.

Growing Wise in Family Life

Do you ever struggle with rushing through your time with God? Spend some unhurried moments with Him today.

_____

_____

_____

GOD SHOWS HIMSELF STRONG

*Store my commands in your heart. If you do this, you will
live many years, and your life will be satisfying.*
PROVERBS 3:1–2

If you focus on the past, it won't be long before complaints start oozing from your lips. You will remember a long-ago time, bathed in a hazy, rosy glow of memory, when something was easier and more comfortable than it is today. And as you compare then and now, I guarantee it, you will grumble.

I do this; so do you. But it's so foolish! We look back nostalgically on what was once a pleasant situation, at which time (even then!) we were looking back longingly on a more pleasant earlier time. That's dumb, isn't it? You may be grumbling right now about your current situation. But chances are good that two years from now you'll be looking back on *this* moment and saying, "Oh, for the good old days! Boy, it was great back then, wasn't it?"

Stop! We live in the light of some dreamy past leisure or pleasure, but in actuality God continues to show Himself strong all along the way.

Moses: A Man of Selfless Dedication

What blessings has God provided in your current situation? Remember
these things when you encounter a difficult season.

_____

_____

_____

IN THE PALM OF GOD'S HAND

For "the earth is the LORD's, and everything in it."
1 CORINTHIANS 10:26

God has the whole world in His hands. Remember the old gospel song? He's got the wind, the rain, the tiny little baby, yes, even you and me in His hands. How easy it is to forget that! And it isn't limited to our geography or our culture, you know. He's got the Middle East in His hands (that's a relief, isn't it?), not to mention Central America and China, Ethiopia and India, Indonesia and Russia—all right there in the palms of His sovereign hands. And while we're at it, He's got our future, our children, our circumstances, our friends, and our foes in His hands . . . within His grasp . . . under His control. Even when imaginary fears slip in like the morning frost to blight our faith, He's there—in charge.

He has yesterday's failures. He has today's challenges. He has tomorrow's surprises right there in His hands. And not one of them causes Him to gasp.

Living on the Ragged Edge

Aren't you glad that nothing catches God off guard and that everything is completely under His control?

_____

_____

_____

EVERYBODY "ACT MEDIUM"

We love each other because he loved us first.
1 JOHN 4:19

The children worked long and hard on their little cardboard shack. It was to be a special spot—a clubhouse, where they could meet together, play, and have fun. Since a clubhouse has to have rules, they came up with three:

- Nobody act big.
- Nobody act small.
- Everybody act medium.

Not bad theology!

In different words, God says the very same thing: "Be humble, thinking of others as better than yourselves" (Philippians 2:3).

Just "act medium." Believable. Honest, human, thoughtful, and down-to-earth.

Day by Day with Charles Swindoll

In a world that says bigger is better, how do you maintain a humble, "medium" attitude?

_____

_____

_____

_____

BLESS THE DAY OF REST

*On the seventh day God had finished his work of
creation, so he rested from all his work.*
GENESIS 2:2

Following the sixth day of creation, the Lord God deliberately stopped working.

He rested. Take special note of that. It wasn't that there was nothing else He could have done. It certainly wasn't because He was exhausted—omnipotence never gets tired! He hadn't run out of ideas, for omniscience knows no mental limitations. He could easily have made many more worlds, created an infinite number of other forms of life, and provided multiple millions of galaxies beyond what He did.

But He didn't. He stopped.

He spent an entire day resting. In fact, He "blessed the seventh day and sanctified it" (Genesis 2:3 NASB), something He did not do on the other six days. He marked this one day off as extremely special. It was like no other. Sounds to me like He made the day on which He rested a "priority" period of time.

Strengthening Your Grip

How are you at rest? What can you begin doing to incorporate more downtime into your schedule?

_____

_____

ACCEPT AND AFFIRM EACH OTHER

The wise are known for their understanding, and pleasant words are persuasive.
PROVERBS 16:21

God commands that we reach out, accept, and affirm one another. This means that we consciously resist the strong current of the stream we are in . . . the one that dictates all those excuses:

- "I'm just too busy."
- "It's not worth the risk."
- "I don't really need anyone."
- "If I reach out, I'll look foolish."

The devil's strategy for our times is working. He has deluded us into believing that we really shouldn't concern ourselves with being our brother's keeper. After all, we have time pressures and work demands (that relentless, fierce determination to be number one), not to mention anxieties prompted by economic uncertainty. And who really needs our help anyway? I'll tell you who—just about every person we meet, that's who.

Strengthening Your Grip

Are you obeying the command to bear one another's burdens? Whom can you reach out to today?

_____

_____

_____

THE WHIRLPOOL OF WICKEDNESS

An evil man is held captive by his own sins; they
are ropes that catch and hold him.
PROVERBS 5:22

What a word picture! We usually think of this situation as applicable only to an unbeliever. But it could just as easily be applied to a Christian who deliberately chooses to disobey his Lord. And instead of seeing the error of his way, he stays in a state of carnality, which grieves the Spirit of God living within him. Carnality occurs when a believer deliberately operates in the strength of his or her own will . . . stubbornly refusing to acknowledge wrong and choosing to walk contrary to the teaching of Scripture. The promptings of God's Spirit are ignored as disobedience and become a lifestyle. Choosing to live like that is like getting caught in a whirlpool. The wickedness intensifies. It gets more treacherous as he goes deeper into it. . . . Like the Prodigal Son, he winds up in misery and filth.

The Grace Awakening

Are you listening to the guidance of the Holy Spirit and seeking to obey the commands of Scripture each day?

_____

_____

_____

GET ETERNITY SECURELY IN PLACE

He has planted eternity in the human heart, but even so, people
cannot see the whole scope of God's work from beginning to end.

ECCLESIASTES 3:11

God has put eternity in our hearts. What in the world does that mean? Well, let me help you with the key word—*eternity*. Let's expand it to mean "curiosity about our future."

God has put within every human being's heart a curiosity about tomorrow . . . an eternal capacity that prompts me to probe, to be intrigued, to search. That explains why your child—just about the time that he or she starts to run around the house and talk—begins to ask questions about tomorrow, about life, and about life beyond. . . . It's the way God made human beings. God has not put eternity in the hearts of animals, only into the hearts of men and women. And since that is true, since we will not find out about tomorrow without God, our pursuit must be of Him.

Living on the Ragged Edge

Have you ever felt the longing for something deeper in your heart? Have you considered that the "more" you seek is more of Him?

_____

_____

_____

A HEART FOR THE TASK

*The eyes of the LORD search the whole earth in order to strengthen
those whose hearts are fully committed to him.*
2 CHRONICLES 16:9

God's choices often seem so illogical from our point of view. We tell ourselves it can't be what He *really* means.

Would you have singled out a sun-withered, eighty-year-old shepherd to face down one of the mightiest kings in the world? Moses had been out to pasture for forty years. He had completely lost touch with his people. He'd been raising a little family, living with and working for his father-in-law. In four decades the man couldn't scrape together enough shekels to build a little place of his own. Admit it, doesn't he seem like a highly unlikely prospect for the job of delivering an entire people group from the clutches of a mighty nation?

God's eyes roam across the planet to find specific individuals whose hearts are just right for a particular task He has in mind. And when He finds them, watch out! He plunges them into the stream of action, upholding them with His mighty hand.

Moses: A Man of Selfless Dedication

Do you feel ill-equipped for a task suddenly placed before you? What if the only thing you need is a heart devoted to the Lord?

_____

_____

AFFECTION AND AFFIRMATION

The father of godly children has cause for joy. What a pleasure to have children who are wise.

PROVERBS 23:24

To you who bear the name "Dad," I cannot impress upon you enough how imperative it is that we show our affection. We can do that in two ways. First, we affirm who our child is; and second, we appreciate what our child does. This twofold assurance, however, must be given in more than words. Affection—the nonverbal communication of closeness—is among the most important experiences we share with our children.

Unaffectionate dads, without ever wishing to do so, can trigger a daughter's promiscuity. All this leads me to write with a great deal of passion, dads . . . *don't hold back your affection!* Demonstrate your feelings of love and acceptance to both sons and daughters. . . . They will love you for it. And, more importantly, they will emulate your example when God gives them a family of their own.

Growing Wise in Family Life

How have you felt the affection of your heavenly Father? What words of affection do you find in Scripture?

_____

_____

_____

TIME WELL SPENT

The heartfelt counsel of a friend is as sweet as perfume and incense.
PROVERBS 27:9

How valuable to *you* are relationships? If you have trouble answering that, I'll help you decide. Stop and think back over the past month or two. How much of your leisure time have you spent developing and enjoying relationships?

Jesus, God's Son, certainly considered the relationship He had with His disciples worth His time. They spent literally *hours* together every single day. They ate together and wept together, and I'm sure they must have laughed together as well. Being God, He really didn't "need" those men. He certainly did not *need* the hassle they created on occasion. But He loved those twelve men. He believed in them.

Whatever leisure time we are able to invest in relationships is time well spent. And when we do, let's keep in mind we are "imitating God," for His Son certainly did.

Strengthening Your Grip

How are you investing in relationships with other believers? Are you living in community?

_____

_____

_____

SAFE IN GOD'S HANDS

*"I would not forget you! See, I have written your
name on the palms of my hands."*
ISAIAH 49:15–16

The Lord has forsaken me. . . . He has walked away. . . . He has totally forgotten me." Ever said that? Of course you have! How about on Monday morning? You've just come off a glorious weekend retreat. Time in the Word. Great worship. . . . Lots of laughter. Meaningful prayer. . . . Then comes eight o'clock Monday morning back home, and your whole *world* caves in. "The Lord's forgotten me. He's completely left the scene."

But God says, "You are written on the palms of My hands. You are continually before Me."

Stop and glance at the palms of your hands. Now, imagine they are God's hands and that you are right there. . . . Our ways remain continually before Him. Not one fleeting moment of life goes by without His knowing exactly where we are, what we're doing, and how we're feeling.

Elijah: A Man of Heroism & Humility

How often do you think of God throughout the day? Does it encourage
you to know that He is always thinking of you?

_____

_____

_____

THE BENEFITS OF SOLITUDE

*Every word of God proves true. He is a shield to
all who come to him for protection.*
PROVERBS 30:5

The Scriptures are replete with references to the value of waiting before the Lord and spending time with Him. When we do, the debris we have gathered during the hurried, busy hours of our day gets filtered out, not unlike the silt that settles where a river widens. With the debris out of the way, we are able to see things more clearly and feel God's nudgings more sensitively.

David frequently underscored the benefits of solitude. I am certain he first became acquainted with this discipline as he kept his father's sheep. Later, during those tumultuous years when King Saul was borderline insane and pursuing him out of jealousy, David found his time with God not only a needed refuge but his means of survival.

God still longs to speak to waiting hearts ... hearts that are quiet before Him.

The Finishing Touch

In a world where the squeaky wheel gets the grease, how can you get quiet before the Lord today?

_____

_____

_____

WHEN GOD SAYS IT WILL BE, IT WILL BE

I know that you can do anything, and no one can stop you.

JOB 42:2

N*o purpose of yours can be thwarted"* (NIV). Remember that conclusion. . . . When God says it will be done, it will be done. If it makes me unhappy? It makes me unhappy. If it hurts? It hurts. If it ruins my reputation? It ruins my reputation.

You want to know who's in charge around here? The One who called the spaces into being, the One who put the clouds in place, the One who established the atmosphere in which we're able to live, the One who separated the seas and the dry land, who gave you breath for your lungs and the ability to think. The One who placed you here, now in time, for His purpose, and the One who with the snap of His divine finger will pull you from life into eternity. Mysterious though our lives may seem, God, and God alone, is in charge.

The Mystery of God's Will

How much of the stress in your life stems from trying to control things that are completely in the hands of God?

_____

_____

_____

_____

THE CENTRAL PIECE OF LIFE'S PUZZLE

"My grace is all you need. My power works best in weakness."
2 CORINTHIANS 12:9

Suffering comes in many forms and degrees, but God's grace is always there to carry us beyond it. I've lived long enough and endured a sufficient number of trials to say without hesitation that only Christ's perspective can replace our resentment with rejoicing. Jesus is the central piece of suffering's puzzle. If we fit Him into place, the rest of the puzzle—no matter how complex and enigmatic—begins to make sense.

Only Christ's salvation can change us from spectators to participants in the unfolding drama of redemption. The scenes will be demanding. Some may be tragic. But only then will we understand the role that suffering plays in our lives. Only then will we be able to tap into hope beyond our suffering.

Hope Again

How have your experiences with suffering made you more like Christ?
Does this change your perspective on pain?

_____

_____

_____

_____

COUNT YOUR BLESSINGS

Let us come to him with thanksgiving. Let us sing psalms of praise to him.
PSALM 95:2

Sometimes when you don't feel like praying, or you're consumed with needing to speak to the Lord but can't gather the words, try that old standby—count your many blessings, count them one by one.

It's amazing how you can get carried away from worries and woes and self-concern when you start naming out loud what you're thankful for. Right away your focus shifts from your needs to the Father's graciousness and love.

Try it!

Day by Day with Charles Swindoll

Take time now to count your blessings. How much better does it make you feel compared to counting your concerns?

_____

_____

_____

_____

_____

_____

153

OUR GUIDE FOR LIFE

"I will guide you along the best pathway for your life.
I will advise you and watch over you."
PSALM 32:8

When we arrive at dilemmas in life and are unable to decipher the right direction to go, if we hope to maintain our joy in the process, we must allow the Lord to be our Guide, our Strength, our Wisdom—our all! It's easy to read those words, but so tough to carry through on them. When we do, however, it's nothing short of remarkable how peaceful and happy we can remain. The pressure is on His shoulders, the responsibility is on Him, the ball is in His court, and an unexplainable joy envelops us.

To be sure, such an unusual method of dealing with dilemmas is rare—there aren't many folks willing to turn the reins over to God—and calls for humility, another rare trait among capable people. But it works! The Lord is a Master at taking our turmoil and revealing the best possible solution to us.

Laugh Again

What decisions, big or small, must you make today? Are you letting the Lord guide your choices?

_____

_____

_____

THE POWER OF RECONCILIATION

"If you forgive those who sin against you, your heavenly Father will forgive you."
MATTHEW 6:14

We cannot be right with God until we are right with one another. The power of reconciliation is stronger than revenge. It is amazing how forgiveness unloads the weapon in the other person's hand. When you reconcile with your brother or sister, it is amazing what it does in both hearts. It is like having your nervous system flushed out. It is like getting over a long-standing fever and cleansing the corruption that has been diseasing your mind. You don't need an attorney for that. You probably don't need a minister or a counselor either. You just need humility. To put it straight, in the final analysis you need guts. Don't wait any longer.

Keep it simple—go and make it right.

Simple Faith

What relationships in your life need some attention? Have you made reconciliation harder than it has to be?

_____

_____

_____

_____

DISCOVER THE DEPTHS OF GOD

Can you discover everything about the Almighty? Such
knowledge is higher than the heavens—and who are you?
JOB 11:7–8

God's ways are not discovered through the normal, humanistic methods of research.

As important and intriguing as divine depths might be, they defy discovery by the natural means of our minds. God reserves these things for those whose hearts are completely His . . . for those who take the time to wait before Him. Only in that way can there be intimacy with the Almighty.

Tragically, precious little in this hurried and hassled age promotes such intimacy. We have become a body of people who look more like a herd of cattle in a stampede than a flock of God beside green pastures and still waters. Our forefathers knew, it seems, how to commune with the Almighty . . . but do we? We must learn anew to think deeply, to worship meaningfully, to meditate unhurriedly.

Intimacy with the Almighty

Is your relationship with the Lord too rushed? Do you simply need to slow down and enjoy Him more?

_____

_____

_____

LET GOD HANDLE IT

"Be still, and know that I am God!"

PSALM 46:10

S it down. That's right, my friend, *sit down!*

You have run far enough. You have stood long enough. You have fought, pushed, and manipulated your way for too many years. God has finally grabbed your attention. He is saying, "Quit! Stop! Let Me handle it! Sit there on the hot sands of the desert where you have brought yourself. Look at what lies next to you. It is a well, full of fresh water." Soon it will be God's delight to bring that bucket up and refresh your soul. Sit still. Stay there. Be quiet.

Cease all the striving. Relax. Be contented by that well, and drink deeply. You are thirstier than you realize.

Moses: A Man of Selfless Dedication

Are you weary? Has the journey been long? God is waiting to refresh your spirit.

_____

_____

_____

_____

_____

_____

TRUE EXCELLENCE

"No one can serve two masters."
MATTHEW 6:24

I f we hope to demonstrate the level of excellence modeled by Jesus Christ, then we'll have to come to terms with the kingdom we are going to serve: the eternal kingdom our Lord told us to seek (Matthew 6:33) or the temporal kingdom of today.

Generally speaking, *God's kingdom is a synonym for God's rule.* Those who choose to live in His kingdom (though still very much alive on planet Earth) choose to live under His authority.

For centuries God has been at work reestablishing His rulership. Jesus' words describe the problem: "No one can serve two masters; for either he will hate the one and love the other, or he will be devoted to one and despise the other" (Matthew 6:24 NASB).

The kingdom is the invisible realm where God rules as supreme author-ity.... Only by letting Him reign in your life can you experience true excellence.

Living Above the Level of Mediocrity

Whom are you serving with your time, talents, and resources? How could you better submit yourself to God's reign?

_____

_____

_____

PAINTED BY GOD'S FINGERS

You take care of the earth and water it. . . . You
crown the year with a bountiful harvest.
PSALM 65:9, 11

S omewhere, miles away, crops push their way toward harvest and waves roar and tumble onto shore. Windswept forests sing their timeless songs, and desert animals scurry in the shadows of cactus and rock.

Within a matter of hours night will fall, the dark sky will glitter with the moon and stars, and sleep will force itself upon us. Life will continue on un-interrupted. Appreciated or not, the canvas of nature will go on being painted by the fingers of God.

In the midst of the offensive noise of our modern world—the people, the cars, the sounds, the smog, the heat, the pressures—there stand those reminders of His deep peace.

The Finishing Touch

Do you struggle to find peace in your life? It is not found in the chaos of the world but in the consistency of God.

_____

_____

_____

_____

STILL, SMALL NUDGES

For the LORD corrects those he loves, just as a father corrects a child in whom he delights.
PROVERBS 3:12

What brings wisdom into our lives? Accepting God's reproofs.
Reproof is from a Hebrew term that means "to correct . . . to convince." I often think of reproofs as God's proddings, those unmistakable nudges, His "still small voice" (1 Kings 19:12 KJV). They are inner promptings designed to correct our ways. They alert us to the fact that we are off course. They communicate, in effect, "My child, that's wrong; change direction!"

These God-given reproofs sometimes appear in Scripture. . . . On other occasions the reproofs come verbally from those who love us.

All of us have sagging character qualities that need attention. To ignore them is to open the gate that leads to disobedience.

Living Beyond the Daily Grind

How do you typically respond to correction? When has the discipline of God put you back on the right path?

_____

_____

_____

_____

WORRY IS WORTHLESS

I look to you for protection. I will hide beneath the shadow
of your wings until the danger passes by.
PSALM 57:1

Worry is a complete waste of energy. It solves nothing. That's why Jesus said, "Can all your worries add a single moment to your life?" (Matthew 6:27). In essence He was saying, "You go to bed tonight and fret and fuss because you're not five feet, eleven inches; you're only five feet, nine inches. But when you wake up in the morning, you're still going to be five feet, nine inches." Worry will never make you stretch! And it won't solve that anxiety on your mind either.

Let me be completely candid here. Do you know why we worry? We have a quiet, hidden, *love* for worry. We enjoy it! When one worry is gone, we replace it with another. There's always a line of worries waiting to get in the door. So as one goes out the back door, we usher in the next one through the front door. We enjoy entertaining them. Worries are our mental and emotional companions. But Jesus says, in effect, that they're worthless!

Perfect Trust

How often have you regretted time spent worrying over things that never happened? Or things that happened anyway? What a waste!

_____

_____

JUNE

AN ATTITUDE OF HUMILITY

Haughtiness goes before destruction; humility precedes honor.
PROVERBS 18:12

Humility is not how you dress, it is not the money you make, it is not where you live, it's not what you drive, it is not even how you look. We're never once commanded by God to "look" humble. Humility is an attitude. It is an attitude of the heart. An attitude of the mind. It is knowing your proper place. Never talking down or looking down because someone may be of a financial level less than yours. It is knowing your role and fulfilling it for God's glory and praise. I repeat, it is an attitude.

It's the attitude Christ had, who emptied Himself of the voluntary and independent use of His divine attributes. There is no quality more godlike than humility.

The place of highest exaltation, as we see in the Lord Jesus Christ, is a place of self-emptying humility. It's not a phony-baloney style of fake piety. It's true humility of mind. It's putting the other person first. . . . It is being like Christ.

Esther: A Woman of Strength and Dignity

How can you begin developing an attitude of humility that makes you more like Christ?

_____

_____

_____

DIVINE RELIEF

So it is God who decides to show mercy. We can neither choose it nor work for it.
ROMANS 9:16

Few feelings bring a greater sense of satisfaction than relief, which Merriam-Webster defines as the "removal or lightening of something oppressive, painful, or distressing."

God calls this divine gift of relief mercy. That's right, *mercy*. It's a twin alongside *grace*.

The essential link between God's grace and our peace is His mercy . . . that is, God's infinite compassion actively demonstrated toward the miserable. Not just pity. Not simply sorrow or an understanding of our plight, but divine relief that results in peace deep within.

The Finishing Touch

How have you experienced the divine relief of the Lord in your life?

_____

_____

_____

_____

_____

BRILLIANT DAYS, BROKEN DAYS

"I will strengthen you and help you. I will hold you
up with my victorious right hand."
ISAIAH 41:10

Our problem isn't that we've failed. Our problem is that we haven't failed enough. We haven't been brought low enough to learn what God wants us to learn.

Remember one of the songs from the '70s we used to sing again and again? It mentioned how we learned to trust in Jesus and to trust in God by going "through it all." Not around it. *Through* it.

Through it *all.* That's the ticket. Through the victories and the failures. . . . Through the brilliant days of accomplishment and the broken days. . . . Through the heady days of laughter and success and those nameless intervals of setback and blank despair. Through it all, He is with us, leading us, teaching us, humbling us, preparing us.

Moses: A Man of Selfless Dedication

What is the greatest lesson you have learned through failure? Did it grow your trust in God?

_____

_____

_____

WATCH THOSE CHOICES!

Commit yourself to instruction; listen carefully to words of knowledge.
PROVERBS 23:12

L iving in truth is making the right choices. Here's what I mean. In the light of truth, you and I are able to see both truth and lie, both light and darkness—that which is simple, pure, and clear and that which is deceptive.

The secret, of course, is making the right choices every day. So? Watch those choices! Watch your decisions!

No married couple suddenly splits. Nobody becomes a cynic overnight. Nobody makes one leap from the pinnacle of praise to the swamp of carnality. Erosion is a slow and silent process based on secret choices. And isn't it remarkable? If you don't stop yourself in the downward process, last week's wrong choice doesn't seem quite so bad this week. In fact, in a month's time it seems like not that bad a choice at all!

Simple Faith

What decisions are you faced with today? Are you seeking God's guidance through prayer and His Word to ensure you're making good choices?

_____

_____

_____

FORGET THE PAST

This means that anyone who belongs to Christ has become a
new person. The old life is gone; a new life has begun!
2 CORINTHIANS 5:17

S ome of the most unhappy people I've ever known are living their lives looking over their shoulders. What a waste! Nothing back there can be changed.
What's in the past? Only two things: great attainments and accomplishments that could make us either proud by reliving them or indifferent by resting
on them . . . or failures and defeats that cannot help but arouse feelings of guilt
and shame. Why in the world would anyone want to return to that quagmire?
I've never been able to figure that one out. By recalling those inglorious, inef-
fective events of yesterday, our energy is sapped for facing the demands of today.
Rehearsing those wrongs, now forgiven in grace, derails and demoralizes us.
There are few joy stealers more insidious than past memories that haunt our
minds. . . . Forget the past!

Laugh Again

Do you find yourself constantly looking back? What is stopping you from
embracing the beauty of today?

_____

_____

_____

MANAGING MISTREATMENT

Instead, you must worship Christ as Lord of your life. And if someone asks about your hope as a believer, always be ready to explain it.
1 PETER 3:15

Anybody can accept a reward graciously, and many people can even take their punishment patiently when they have done something wrong. But how many people are equipped to handle mistreatment after they've done right? Only Christians are equipped to do that.

When we think a wrong has been done to us that we don't deserve, we can respond, "Lord, You're with me right now. You are here, and You have Your reasons for what is happening. You will not take advantage of me. You're much too kind to be cruel. You're much too good to be unjust. You care for me too much to let this get out of hand. Take charge. Use my integrity to defend me. Give me the grace to stay calm. Control my emotions. Be Lord over my present situation." In such a prayer, we "sanctify Christ as Lord" in our hearts (1 Peter 3:15 NASB).

Hope Again

Are you being judged wrongly or suffering unjustly? Do you trust the Lord to be your defender?

_____

_____

_____

A CAVALIER CULTURE

A real friend sticks closer than a brother.

PROVERBS 18:24

A hurry-up lifestyle results in a throwaway culture. Things that should be lasting and meaningful are sacrificed on the altar of the temporary and superficial.

The major fallout in such a setting is the habit of viewing relationships casually. This cavalier attitude cripples society in various ways:

Friends walk away instead of work through.

Partnerships dissolve rather than solve.

Neighbors no longer visit and relax together.

The aged are resented, not honored.

Husbands and wives divorce rather than persevere.

Children are brushed aside rather than nourished.

Relationships! Never sell them short. If we'll slow down the hurry-up lifestyle for a moment and pause to catch our breath, we'll realize the need to call a halt to our throwaway culture.

Growing Wise in Family Life

Has the rush of life resulted in a lack of real relationships in your life? In whom do you need to invest more time and energy?

_____

_____

LET GO AND LET GOD

Don't be afraid. Just stand still and watch the LORD rescue you today.
EXODUS 14:13

We Americans use a number of words to describe a predicament. If you're from the East Coast, you probably know about "being in a pinch." If you like to cook, you know the phrases "in a jam" or "in a pickle." If you're from the South, you're "between a rock and a hard place." . . . It may be that right now you find yourself in a predicament.

And what should your response be?

Most people are prone to say, "God helps those who help themselves." People think that despicable saying comes from the Bible, but it doesn't. It's from the pit. No, God helps *the helpless!* As long as we're helping ourselves, who needs God? It's when we reach the end of our tether, and we're dangling out in space, that we finally cry out, "God, help me!" And God says, "I will. *Let go.*"

Letting go works against human nature. But God wants us to do just that—to freefall into His everlasting arms and trust completely in Him.

Moses: A Man of Selfless Dedication

Have you found yourself believing the lie that you must get yourself out of the mess you're in? What if you turned to God instead?

_____

_____

_____

THE END OF THE STORY

Finishing is better than starting. . . . Wisdom is even better when you have money. . . . Wisdom and money can get you almost anything.

ECCLESIASTES 7:8, 11, 12

The end of a matter is better than its beginning" (NIV). That makes sense, doesn't it? You see, the end of a matter is maximum reality. Those little idealistic dreams have ended. The whole truth is on display. . . . The complete picture has developed. Once we reach the end, we know the whole story, and that is better than the beginning of a matter where desires lack substance.

I had a grandfather tell me recently that he plans to record a lot of his thoughts because, he said, "I don't know how long I'm gonna live and I don't know how long I'll have my mind, so I'm gonna record some important counsel and let my grandchildren listen to it later on."

The most influential man in my life was my mother's father. I can still hear his wise counsel. Such counsel is better than most advice given to a child because it is end-of-the-matter information coming from one who has been seasoned with wisdom.

Living on the Ragged Edge

Whose "end-of-the-matter" wisdom has made an impact on your life? Do you have some counsel that others need to hear?

_____

_____

LEISURE IS FREE

A little extra sleep, a little more slumber, a little folding of the hands to rest.
PROVERBS 24:33

Please understand that leisure is more than idle free time not devoted to paid occupations. Some of the most valuable work done in the world has been done at leisure . . . and never paid for in cash. Leisure is free activity. Labor is compulsory activity. In leisure, we do what we like, but in labor we do what we must. In our labor we meet the objective needs and demands of others—our employer, the public, people who are impacted by and through our work. But in leisure we scratch the subjective itches within ourselves. In leisure our minds are liberated from the immediate, the necessary. As we incorporate leisure into the mainstream of our world, we gain perspective. We lift ourselves above the grit and grind of mere existence.

Interestingly, leisure comes from the Latin word *licere*, which means "to be permitted." If we are ever going to inculcate leisure into our otherwise utilitarian routine, we must give ourselves permission to do so.

Strengthening Your Grip

What leisure activity brings you the most joy? Do you allow yourself time in your schedule to enjoy it?

_____

_____

_____

ALIGNED TO GOD'S WILL

The seeds of good deeds become a tree of life; a wise person wins friends.
PROVERBS 11:30

I f we were asked to respond with yes or no to the question, all of us would say, "Yes, I want to know [God's] will." But *doing* God's will is another matter entirely, because almost without exception it requires risk and adjustment and change. We don't like that. Even using those words makes us squirm. Experiencing the reality of them is even worse. We love the familiar. We love the comfortable. We love something we can control—something we can get our arms around. Yet the closer we walk with the Lord, the less control we have over our own lives, and the more we must abandon to Him. To give Him our wills and to align our wills to His will requires the abandonment of what we prefer, what we want or what we would choose.

The Mystery of God's Will

Do you desire God's will and delight in obeying it? Why is it sometimes a struggle to choose His will over your own?

_____

_____

_____

_____

_____

A RAT IN THE CORNER OF LIFE

"What is the price of two sparrows—one copper coin? But not a single sparrow can fall to the ground without your Father knowing it."
MATTHEW 10:29

Maybe you have a worry related to some simple, daily problem that eats away at your peace, like a rat in the corner of your life. It just gnaws and gnaws and gnaws. You can't seem to get out from under it. Maybe it was a foolish mistake you made and you're paying for it.

One problem with worry is that *it makes you forget your worth*. Worry makes you feel worthless, forgotten, and unimportant. That's why Jesus says that we are worth much more than the birds of the air who neither worry nor die of hunger because their heavenly Father feeds them (Matthew 6:26). They enjoy what's there. If God is able to sustain the lesser creatures, won't He sustain the greater? Maybe you're worried about things that seem important in your life. Yet your heavenly Father knows what is essential better than you do. And you are worth so much that He is taking things one at a time, dealing with more important things right now in your life.

Perfect Trust

Have you forgotten how valuable you are to your heavenly Father? Do you trust Him to handle the hard things in your life?

_____

_____

DEFLATING PRIDE

*"Consider the rock from which you were cut, the
quarry from which you were mined."*

ISAIAH 51:1

In the Hebrew text, the word *quarry* actually refers to "a hole." The King James Version doesn't miss it far: "the hole of the pit whence ye are digged." Never forget "the hole of the pit."

What excellent advice! Before we get all enamored with our high-and-mighty importance, it's a good idea to take a backward glance at the "hole of the pit" from which Christ lifted us. And let's not just *think* about it; let's admit it. Our "hole of the pit" has a way of keeping us all on the same level—recipients of grace. And don't kid yourself, even those who are extolled and admired have "holes" from which they were dug.

- With Moses, it was murder.
- With Peter, it was public denial.
- With Rahab, it was prostitution.

The next time we're tempted to become puffed up by our own importance, let's just look back to the pit from which we were dug. It has a way of deflating our pride.

Strengthening Your Grip

Do you ever take the time to remember where you were when the Lord found you? Are you amazed at how far He has brought you?

THE SOUL BELONGS TO GOD

Then I will rejoice in the LORD. I will be glad because he rescues me.
PSALM 35:9

Nothing physical touches the soul. Nothing external satisfies our deepest inner needs. Remember that! The soul belongs to God. He alone can satisfy us in that realm.

The soul possesses an inescapable God-shaped vacuum. And not until He invades and fills it can we be at peace within—which is another way of saying, "If God isn't in first place, you can't handle success." If God fills your soul, if God fills your mind, if God satisfies your spirit, there is no problem whatsoever with prosperity. You've got it all put together. Your priorities will be right, and you will know how to handle your life so you can impact the maximum number of people. If He prospers you, if He entrusts you with material success and you continue walking with Him, God can use you mightily in His plan. Furthermore, if you lose it all, He can give you what it takes to handle the loss and start all over again.

Living on the Ragged Edge

Is God first in your life? How does this better enable you to handle both suffering and success?

_____

_____

_____

WE WANT RELIEF

I love the LORD because he hears my voice and my prayer for mercy.
Because he bends down to listen, I will pray as long as I have breath!
PSALM 116:1–2

D o you ever find yourself saying something like this? "Lord, I give You my life, but I'm weary to death of this irritation, this person, this circumstance, this uncomfortable situation. I feel trapped, Lord. I want relief—I must have relief! And if You don't bring it soon . . . well, I've had it. I feel like walking away from it all."

You may walk, my friend, but there are no shortcuts. Here's a better plan: reach for the hand of your Guide! He is Lord of the desert. Even your desert. The most precious object of God's love is His child in the desert. If it were possible, you mean more to Him during this time than at any other time. . . . You are His beloved student taking His toughest courses. He loves you with an infinite amount of love.

Moses: A Man of Selfless Dedication

When have you prayed earnestly to be out of a difficult situation but, looking back, realized the beauty of walking with the Lord through it?

_____

_____

_____

A DAD'S GREATEST GIFT

My children, listen when your father corrects you.
Pay attention and learn good judgment.
PROVERBS 4:1

Dad, is it possible you've gotten overly committed, so involved in your work or some away-from-home project or hobby that it is draining your time and energy with your family? I understand, believe me, I do.

Instead of challenging fathers to give of themselves, our cultural system encourages them to give the stuff their increased salaries can buy—a better education, a membership at the club, material possessions, nicer homes, extra cars.... But what about dad himself? And that priceless apprenticeship learned in his presence? . . . It's gotten lost in the shuffle.

C'mon, dads, let's lead a revolt! Let's refuse to take our cues from the system any longer. Let's start saying no to more and more of the things that pull us further and further away from the ones who need us the most. Let's remember that the greatest earthly gifts we can provide are our presence and influence while we live and a magnificent memory of our lives once we're gone.

Growing Wise in Family Life

Have your priorities gotten a little out of line? Do you understand that the most precious thing you have to offer your family is yourself?

_____

_____

FACE-TO-FACE WITH GOD

God will judge us for everything we do, including
every secret thing, whether good or bad.
ECCLESIASTES 12:14

I f God says that He will bring every act to judgment . . . I know He will. I
don't know His method and, frankly, that doesn't bother me. What ought to
bother us is that He will do it! . . . Somehow in God's own timing and in God's
own way, He will cause there to be a replay of our lives. . . . It makes a lot of
sense to me that the One who made us has every right to hold us accountable.

We cannot live the life of an irresponsible playboy and get away with it.
We aren't free to run wild and wink in God's direction, thinking that, no matter what, the big Teddy Bear in the sky will yawn, pat us on the head, and say,
"Everything is going to be just fine." No, it doesn't work like that. Our ragged-
edge journey is headed for a sudden stop. And all alone, standing face-to-face
with God in that epochal moment, we will give an account of the life we have
lived.

Sober, serious thought!

Living on the Ragged Edge

Do you live each day with an understanding that you will one day give an
account for the choices you've made?

_____

_____

HOLD ON TO GOD'S HAND

Search for the LORD and for his strength; continually seek him.
PSALM 105:4

Discovering and embracing God's will leads us to make major adjustments. And that requires us to release and risk—releasing the familiar and risking whatever the future may bring. That's the bottom line of fleshing out God's will.

We are only finite human beings. We can only see the present and the past. The future is a little frightening to us. So we need to hold on to God's hand and trust Him to calm our fears. And at those times when we're stubborn and resisting and God shakes us by the shoulders to get our attention, we're reminded that we don't call our own shots, that God has a plan for us, mysterious though it may seem, and we want to be in the center of it.

All the risks notwithstanding, that's still the safest place on earth to be.

The Mystery of God's Will

Do you find yourself sometimes fighting for control of your life only to discover that you have no idea what to do next? Let God have the reins.

_____

_____

_____

_____

SENSITIVE RATHER THAN STRONG

*For husbands, this means love your wives, just as Christ
loved the church. He gave up his life for her.*

EPHESIANS 5:25

God's goal for us as husbands is to be sensitive rather than to prove how strong and macho we are. We need to love our wives, listen to them, adapt to their needs. We need to say no to more and more in our work so we can say yes to more and more in our homes . . . so we can say yes to the needs of our children and our families. (How else will your children learn what it means to be a good husband and father?)

Mind you, this is not to be a smothering kind of attention—the kind that says a husband is so insecure he cannot let his wife out of his sight. Instead, this is the kind of love that means your wife can't come back fast enough to your arms.

Hope Again

How has the world twisted what it means to be a man? What are some godly traits that the world may not understand?

_____

_____

_____

_____

_____

GOD'S MYSTERIOUS PLAN

"I am the LORD; there is no other God."
ISAIAH 45:5

There are occasions when we are surprised by God's decreed will . . . like when we get the results back from our physical exam and the MRI reveals a tumor we had no idea was there. . . . Or when the stock market plunges in one day to a ten-year, record-setting low.

It may seem to many that the One who made us is too far removed to concern Himself with such tiny details of life on this old globe. But that is not the case. His mysterious plan is running its course right on schedule, exactly as He decreed it.

This world is not out of control, spinning wildly through space. Nor are earth's inhabitants at the mercy of some blind, random fate. When God created the world and set the stars in space, He also established the course of this world and His plan for humanity.

The Mystery of God's Will

Is your default response to earthly troubles panic or a certainty that the Lord is still completely in control of His creation?

_____

_____

_____

_____

THE HEARTBEAT OF THE HOME

If you stop listening to instruction, my child, you
will turn your back on knowledge.
PROVERBS 19:27

The birth of a child is not taken lightly by the Lord. Each one is significant. Each one is viewed by God as a transfer of love from His heart to the couple receiving the gift.

God never wastes parents. He doesn't inadvertently "dump" kids haphazardly into homes. Nor does He deliver "accidents" into our lives. It is exceedingly important that families place the same significance on children that God does. Again, this is contrary to the mentality of many people in our society today. We are considered as somewhere between weird and ignorant if we have this kind of attitude toward children, especially if we have a large number of them.

It is axiomatic. Healthy, well-disciplined, loving homes produce people who make a nation peaceful and strong. As the family goes, so goes the nation. When you boil it down to the basics, the pulse of an entire civilization is determined by the heartbeat of its homes.

Strengthening Your Grip

How can you help the children in your life (within your home or community) grow up and become all that God intends them to become?

_____

_____

HUMBLE IN HEART

"Take my yoke upon you. Let me teach you, because I am humble and gentle at heart, and you will find rest for your souls."
MATTHEW 11:29

What is the most Christlike attitude on earth? Think before you answer too quickly. I am certain many would answer *love*. That is understandable, for He did indeed love to the uttermost. Others might say *patience*. Again, not a bad choice. I find no evidence of impatience or anxious irritability as I study His life. *Grace* would also be a possibility. No man or woman ever modeled or exhibited the grace that He demonstrated right up to the moment He breathed His last.

As important as those traits may be, however, they are not the ones Jesus Himself referred to when He described Himself for the only time in Scripture.... "I am gentle and humble in heart" (Matthew 11:29 NASB), which might best be summed up in one word: *unselfish*. According to Jesus' testimony, that is the most Christlike attitude we can demonstrate.

Laugh Again

What one trait would you say defines you as a person? How does it compare to Christ's description of Himself?

_____

_____

A MESSAGE FOR THE MARKETPLACE

Whatever you do, do well.
ECCLESIASTES 9:10

I'm just maverick enough to say that I think fewer Christian ought to be going into the ministry and more should be going into business and into occupations that have nothing to do with the vocational Christian service. I don't see life divided into public and private, secular and sacred. It's all an open place of service before our God. My hope is to see . . . a group of Christians who will infiltrate our society—in fact, our entire world—with a pure, beautiful message of grace and honesty in the marketplace.

Recently I had a delightful talk with a keen-thinking young man . . . at our church. As we visited, I asked him about his future plans. "Well, I've just graduated from law school," he said. When I asked about how he hoped to use his training, he said, "I want to be a man of integrity who practices law." What refreshing words! They reflected the right priority.

Simple Faith

Do you view your whole life as a place of ministry? How can you honor the Lord in all that you do?

_____

_____

_____

FAITH FOR THE FUTURE

And I rejoice that you are living as you should and
that your faith in Christ is strong.
COLOSSIANS 2:5

The nature of the beast within all of us resists change. Even though our past has been painful and in some ways unrewarding and perhaps even unproductive, it would be interesting to know how many of us would rather return to our past than face the uncertainty of our future. Being creatures of habit, we would rather have the security of our yesterday than the uncertainty of our tomorrow.

But it's the uncertainty of our future that really strengthens our faith. I mean, if we knew what it was all about, then it would take no faith. All it would take is obedience. If you knew what was going to happen in the next ten years of your life, what kind of faith would it take to walk that path?

It's the mystery of it all that gives it the power, the mystery of the whole process called God's working that makes the power so magnificent.

Dropping Your Guard

Are you preoccupied with the beauty or brokenness of yesterday? Do you live with fear of the future? What would happen if you just focused on today?

_____

_____

A JOYFUL HEART

You have given me greater joy.
PSALM 4:7

We need to lighten up! Yes, spirituality and fun do go well together. Scripture speaks directly to this issue, you know: "A joyful heart makes a cheerful face, but when the heart is sad, the spirit is broken" (Proverbs 15:13 NASB).

We're not talking about a person's face here as much as we are about the heart. Internal joy goes public. We can't hide it. The face takes its cue from an inside signal.

A well-developed sense of humor reveals a well-balanced personality. . . . The ability to get a laugh out of everyday situations is a safety valve. It rids us of tensions and worries that could otherwise damage our health.

You think I'm exaggerating the benefits? If so, maybe you've forgotten another proverb: "A joyful heart is good medicine" (Proverbs 17:22 NASB). What is it that brings healing to the emotions, healing to the soul? A joyful heart!

Living Above the Level of Mediocrity

Who do you know exudes joy when you're around them? How does it feel to be in their presence?

_____

_____

_____

GOD'S WILL AND WAYS

As the deer longs for streams of water, so I long for you, O God.
PSALM 42:1

Godliness is something below the surface of a life, deep down in the realm of attitude—an attitude toward God Himself.

The longer I think about this, the more I believe that a person who is godly is one whose heart is sensitive toward God, one who takes God seriously. . . . The godly individual hungers and thirsts after God. In the words of the psalmist, the godly person has a soul that "pants" for the living God (Psalm 42:1–2 NASB).

Godly people possess an attitude of willing submission to God's will and ways. Whatever He says goes. And whatever it takes to carry it out is the very thing the godly desire to do.

The Finishing Touch

What do you thirst for in this life? How would you go about increasing your desire for God?

_____

_____

_____

_____

_____

OUR WEAKNESS, HIS STRENGTH

Wait patiently for the LORD. Be brave and courageous.
Yes, wait patiently for the LORD.
PSALM 27:14

Let's look at that term *wait*. It is from the Hebrew verb *kah-wah*, meaning "to twist, stretch." The noun form means "line, cord, thread." A vivid picture emerges here. It is a verb describing the making of a strong, powerful rope or cord by twisting and weaving ourselves so tightly around the Lord that our weaknesses and frail characteristics are replaced by His power and unparalleled strength. It describes very literally the truth of what has been termed the "exchanged life." As we wait on God, our weakness is exchanged for His strength.

Strength and courage are developed *during* a trial, not after it is over.

Living Beyond the Daily Grind

Can you recall a time when you endured a trial and knew that only the Lord could have pulled you through?

_____

_____

_____

_____

WALKING WITH GOD

It is better to take refuge in the Lord than to trust in people.

PSALM 118:8

Walking with God is the most exciting and rewarding of all experiences on earth. I should add, it is also the most difficult. I don't think I've ever met an exception to the rule, that those who walk closest to God are those who, like Jesus, become acquainted with trials and testings. God takes us through struggles and difficulties so that we might become increasingly more committed to Him.

God may be leading you somewhere . . . that doesn't make much sense. I want to encourage you: don't try to make sense out of it. Just go. If God leads you to stay in a difficult situation and you have peace that you are to stay, don't analyze it. Stay. Do your part. Do what He tells you to do, for His promises often hinge on obedience.

You can walk with Him in perfect trust. That's your part.

Perfect Trust

Do you find yourself obsessing over the "why" of a situation? Could it be that God just wants you to trust and obey?

_____

_____

_____

SELF-CONTROL IS INNER STRENGTH

But the Holy Spirit produces this kind of fruit in our lives: love, joy, peace, patience, kindness, goodness, faithfulness, gentleness, and self-control.
GALATIANS 5:22–23

Every one of us has gotten angry and lost our tempers, only to regret it. Every one of us has allowed our schedules to get so overloaded that, looking back over the week, we must admit to ourselves, if we're honest, we've not stopped to pray even once. Every one of us has eaten too much, even when we swore we wouldn't. Who hasn't fought yet again the old battle with lust or greed or materialism or anger or envy?

There is an answer to this daily dilemma, a solution that is easy to identify. There is a secret to holding back.

"Self-control" . . . that's the key . . . that's the answer.

The best synonym for self-control is "discipline." . . . Self-control means "inner strength."

The fruit of the Spirit is self-control. Self-control frees us from slavery. Self-control stops bad habits. It checks us. It halts us.

Esther: A Woman of Strength and Dignity

Have you told yourself that you're too weak to resist some area of temptation? As a believer, you have the fruit of self-control at your disposal.

JULY

DILIGENCE AND FAITHFULNESS

Worship the LORD with gladness. Come before him, singing with joy.
PSALM 100:2

S ervanthood implies diligence, faithfulness, loyalty, and humility.
Servants don't compete . . . or grandstand . . . or polish their image . . .
or grab the limelight. They know their job, they admit their limitations, they do
what they do quietly and consistently.

Servants cannot control anyone or everything, and they shouldn't try.

Servants cannot change or "fix" people.

Servants cannot concern themselves with who gets the credit.

Let's serve . . . in the name of Jesus.

The Finishing Touch

Do you serve with the expectation of reward or recognition? What if you
gave no thought to anything except honoring the Lord?

_____

_____

_____

_____

_____

_____

ONLY CHARACTER ENDURES

I have acted with integrity; I have trusted in the LORD without wavering.

PSALM 26:1

Nothing speaks louder or more powerfully than a life of integrity. Absolutely nothing! Nothing stands the test like solid character. You can handle the blast like a steer in a blizzard. The ice may form on your horns, but you keep standing against the wind and the howling, raging storm because Christ is at work in your spirit. Character will always win the day. As Horace Greeley wrote: "Fame is a vapor, popularity an accident, riches take wing, and only character endures."

There is no more eloquent and effective defense than a life lived continually and consistently in integrity. It possesses invincible power to silence your slanderers.

Hope Again

At the end of it all, when health and wealth are forgotten and gone, have you lived in a way that made a difference in the kingdom?

_____

_____

_____

_____

_____

HURRIED, HARRIED HOMES?

Know the state of your flocks, and put your heart into caring for your herds.
PROVERBS 27:23

What's the atmosphere like in your home these days? . . . Are you in danger of raising a "hurried child"? Capture some time this week and take an honest look at the quality of childhood your family lifestyle is providing for your little ones. What will be memorable to your kids when they, as adults, look back on the early years? Will it all seem like a high-pressure blur to them . . . one long, breathless marathon? Have you allowed television to snatch up much of your children's unscheduled minutes . . . and *hours?*

Seeking God's wisdom, ask yourselves, "What can we do as mom and dad to encourage our kids to enjoy being *kids?*" Are you creating an atmosphere of relaxation and flexibility . . . or do the words *hurry* and *rigidity* better characterize your home? Any plans for a relaxed family vacation in the works? . . . As you plan, remember that childhood is an infinitely precious commodity. Your children will only grow up once.

Growing Wise in Family Life

How can you help your children slow down? Are their schedules too full? Is there time for imagination and creativity?

_____

_____

_____

THE BEAUTY OF GOD'S HOLINESS

*Holy, holy, holy is the Lord God, the Almighty—the one
who always was, who is, and who is still to come.*

We live in a day of pitifully shallow concepts of God. Some of today's contemporary Christian music leaves the impression that God is our buddy—a great pal to have in a pinch. . . . One pop song asks, "What if God were just a slob like us?" That is not the biblical view of God. That is man's feeble attempt to make God *relevant*.

Do you hear the cheap twang of such a concept of God? These small ideas of Him diminish the beauty of His holiness.

The Puritans, that rigorous people of old, possessed a solidly biblical concept of God. Do you know why it is so crucial for us to recover such a respectful understanding? Because a shallow view of God leads to a shallow life. Cheapen God and you cheapen life itself. Treat God superficially, and you become superficial.

Moses: A Man of Selfless Dedication

How is the world guilty of trying to bring God down to man's level? What does His Word say about His holiness?

_____

_____

_____

Undeserved Kindness

*We believe that we are all saved the same way, by
the undeserved grace of the Lord Jesus.*
Acts 15:11

I f you have traveled to London, you have perhaps seen royalty. If so, you may have noticed sophistication, aloofness, distance. On occasion, royalty in England will make the news because someone in the ranks of nobility will stop, kneel down, and touch or bless a commoner. That is grace. There is nothing in the commoner that deserves being noticed or touched or blessed by the royal family. But because of grace in the heart of the queen, there is the desire at that moment to pause, to stoop, to touch, even to bless.

To show grace is to extend favor or kindness to one who doesn't deserve it and can never earn it. Receiving God's acceptance by grace always stands in sharp contrast to earning it on the basis of works. Every time the thought of grace appears, there is the idea of its being undeserved. In no way is the recipient getting what he or she deserves. Favor is being extended simply out of the goodness of the heart of the giver.

The Grace Awakening

Aren't you grateful that God doesn't give you what you deserve? How do you see evidence of God's grace in your life?

_____

_____

STOP THE BLAME GAME

People who conceal their sins will not prosper, but if they
confess and turn from them, they will receive mercy.
PROVERBS 28:13

Let's not kid ourselves. When we deliberately choose not to stay positive and deny joy a place in our lives, we'll usually gravitate in one of two directions, sometimes both—the direction of blame or self-pity.

The aggressive attitude reacts to circumstances with blame. We blame ourselves or someone else, or God, or if we can't find a tangible scapegoat, we blame "fate." What an absolute waste! When we blame ourselves, we multiply our guilt, we rivet ourselves to the past (another "dangling" unchangeable), and we decrease our already low self-esteem. If we choose to blame God, we cut off our single source of power. Doubt replaces trust, and we put down roots of bitterness that can make us cynical. If we blame others, we enlarge the distance between us and them. . . . We settle for something much less than God ever intended. And on top of all that, we do not find relief!

Strengthening Your Grip

Have you ever considered that joy is a choice you make? What would it look like for you to choose it today?

_____

_____

_____

WELCOME WISE REBUKES

An open rebuke is better than hidden love!
PROVERBS 27:5

Hearing a wise person's rebuke is far better than humming a fool's song. That's the idea. Most of us fail to hear the rebukes of the wise. Sometimes the wise person is a boss who attempts to evaluate our job. At other times it's a parent who pulls us up close, in one of those nose-to-nose encounters, and tells us some things we need to hear. But we find such occasions difficult to bear.

Are we listening to the rebuke of the wise? Sometimes the wise rebuke comes from a former mate. Or the wise person could be a pastor, or a therapist, or a physician, or an attorney. We must be open and willing to learn from rebukes.

Living on the Ragged Edge

When has someone loved you enough to speak a hard truth to you?

_____

_____

_____

_____

_____

STUBBORN SOMETIMES

*Do not be like a senseless horse or mule that needs
a bit and bridle to keep it under control.*
PSALM 32:9

You've heard of God's children referred to as sheep. It isn't a bad picture, all things considered. The image conjures up visions of green pastures, still waters, and a gentle Shepherd, keeping watch over the flock.

But He also refers to us as mules. Sometimes, I think that's a better analogy.

Don't be like a balky mule! Don't be stubborn when God speaks. Don't continually fight and resist Him. Don't keep running away from Him so that He can't speak to you. Don't force Him to lasso you before you'll let Him draw near.

Why do we resist such a magnificent God who loves us? It makes no sense!

Moses: A Man of Selfless Dedication

Think about your attitude lately. Do you resemble a sheep remaining close to the Shepherd or a stubborn mule?

_____

_____

_____

_____

YOUR FINGERPRINTS OR GOD'S?

The way of the LORD is a stronghold to those with
integrity, but it destroys the wicked.

PROVERBS 10:29

You cannot sow a fleshly seed and reap a spiritual plant. You cannot plant a carnal act and grow spiritual fruit. If you manipulate and connive and scheme and lie to get yourself to the top, don't thank God for the promotion! God knows, as you know, that you maneuvered and pulled strings. . . . So when you get that bigger office and the key to the executive washroom, don't give Him the credit. He doesn't want it. Your fingerprints are all over that scheme, not His.

At times we say to the Lord, "Thanks for that, Father." And the Lord must answer back, "Who? Me? I didn't pull that off. That was *your* doing." . . . You fudge on your income tax, get a nice refund, and thank Him for the extra cash you can give to the building fund.

It doesn't work that way, friend. He says to you, "This isn't My doing. This is your plan."

Moses: A Man of Selfless Dedication

Have you ever been guilty of giving God "credit" for something that was your doing? Or taking credit for something that came from His hand?

_____

_____

DEVELOPING SECURE CHILDREN

The man who loves wisdom brings joy to his father.
PROVERBS 29:3

If parents were to ask me, "What is the greatest gift we could give our young child?" I would answer rather quickly: a sensitive spirit. That is especially rare among busy parents who live under the demands of hurried schedules, constantly doing battle with the tyranny of the urgent. Nevertheless, my counsel to you would be, give your child the time it takes to find out how he or she is put together. Help your child know who he or she is. Discuss those things with your children. Help them know themselves so that they learn to love and accept themselves as they are. Then, as they move into a society that seems committed to pounding them into another shape, they will remain true to themselves, secure in their independent walk with God.

I have begun to realize that secure, mature people are best described in fifteen words. They know who they are. . . . They like who they are. . . . They are who they are. They are *real*.

Growing Wise in Family Life

What specific traits has God placed in your children? Are you helping them see and embrace them?

_____

_____

_____

THE FAIREST FLOWER

Lord, my heart is not proud; my eyes are not haughty. I don't concern myself with matters too great or too awesome for me to grasp.

PSALM 131:1

Genuine humility isn't something we can announce very easily. To claim this virtue is, as a rule, to forfeit it. Humility is the fairest and rarest flower that blooms. Put it on display and instantly it wilts and loses its fragrance! . . . No, humility is not something to be announced. It simply belongs in one's life, in the private journal of one's walk with God.

There are two simple and quick ways God says the true condition of the heart is revealed. The first is through the eyes and the second is through the mouth (Luke 6:45). . . . Keen counselors and wise people are careful to listen to words (what is said as well as what *isn't* said) and watch the eyes of others. You soon discover that the heart is like a well and the eyes and tongue are like buckets that draw water from the same well. If true humility is not in the heart, the eyes will show it.

Living Beyond the Daily Grind II

How do you interact with people around you? Do you have eyes that are haughty or humble?

_____

_____

_____

God Is All in All

The king's heart is like a stream of water directed by
the Lord; he guides it wherever he pleases.
Proverbs 21:1

God rules, God reigns. God, and God alone. And His way is right. It leads to His glory.

Deep within the hearts of men and women, even though most would never acknowledge it, is the realization that we really don't have the final answer. There is this little hidden clause tucked away in the deep recesses of most thinking minds that says, "There may be a God after all."

When we take this to the ultimate future for humanity, God is sovereignly in charge. One second after they die, the men and women who have rejected and resisted the Lord for years will step into eternity. One second . . . and they will be totally at a loss to determine their future. God's sovereignty steps over their lives and sets forth His decree, "That God may be all in all" (1 Corinthians 15:28 KJV).

The Mystery of God's Will

Is there someone in your life who needs to be reminded that God is all in all? Maybe it's you?

_____

_____

_____

LET GOD BUILD YOUR HOUSE

Unless the LORD builds a house, the work of the builders is wasted.
PSALM 127:1

Here's the idea. During those all-important early months and years of marriage, make sure that the Lord your God is the heart and center of your family! If He is not, the whole experience is a study in futility—a wasted, empty, counterproductive effort. It will all be in vain. He doesn't have in mind a home that hangs a lot of religious mottos on the walls or a couple that simply goes to church regularly or offers up a quick prayer before meals or places a big Bible on the living room coffee table. No, the essential ingredient is "the Lord."

A family gets started on the right foot when Jesus Christ is in each life (husband and wife are both born again), and when the lengthening shadow of His lordship pervades that relationship. When a couple makes Christ a vital part of their life, in the terms of the psalm, that's when "the LORD builds a house."

Strengthening Your Grip

Regardless of how long you've been married (or even if you're single), it's not too late to ask the Lord to build or rebuild your house.

NOTHING HELPS LIKE HOPE

Let us hold tightly without wavering to the hope we affirm,
for God can be trusted to keep his promise.
HEBREWS 10:23

H ope is a wonderful gift from God, a source of strength and courage in the face of life's harshest trials.

When we are trapped in a tunnel of misery, hope points to the light at the end.

When we are overworked and exhausted, hope gives us fresh energy.

When we are discouraged, hope lifts our spirits.

When we are tempted to quit, hope keeps us going.

When we struggle with a crippling disease or a lingering illness, hope helps us persevere beyond the pain.

When we fear the worst, hope brings reminders that God is still in control.

When we are forced to sit back and wait, hope gives us the patience to trust.

Put simply, when life hurts and dreams fade, nothing helps like hope.

Hope Again

Are you clinging tightly to hope right now? What promises are you trusting God to keep?

_____

_____

THE PURSUIT OF HAPPINESS

For to me, living means living for Christ, and dying is even better.

PHILIPPIANS 1:21

When money is our objective, we must live in fear of losing it, which makes us paranoid and suspicious.

When fame is our aim, we become competitive lest others upstage us, which makes us envious.

When power and influence drive us, we become self-serving and strong-willed, which makes us arrogant.

And when possessions become our god, we become materialistic, thinking enough is never enough, which makes us greedy.

All these pursuits fly in the face of contentment . . . and joy.

Only Christ can satisfy, whether we have or don't have, whether we are known or unknown, whether we live or die. . . . The pursuit of happiness is the cultivation of a Christ-centered, Christ-controlled life.

Laugh Again

Are you pursuing things that can be lost and taken or seeking the satisfaction found only in Christ?

_____

_____

_____

HAND-IN-HAND

Then make me truly happy by agreeing wholeheartedly with each other,
loving one another, and working together with one mind and purpose.
PHILIPPIANS 2:2

I t is only when I *share* life's experiences with others that I can enjoy them or endure them to the greatest advantage. This is what the early Christians did. They learned quickly that survival would go hand-in-hand with fellowship.

You see, having a relationship calls for being in fellowship with others, and that cannot be done very easily at arm's length. It implies getting in touch, feeling the hurts, being an instrument of encouragement and healing. Fences must come down. Masks need to come off. Welcome signs need to be hung outside the door. Keys to the locks in our lives must be duplicated and distributed. Bridges need to be lowered that allow others to cross the moat and then share our joys and our sorrows.

Dropping Your Guard

What are your fears involved in fellowship? Do you need to let them go and allow yourself to be known?

_____

_____

_____

_____

THE BLESSED LIFE

"God blesses those whose hearts are pure, for they will see God."
MATTHEW 5:8

What is meant by *blessed?* Some say it is little more than a synonym for "happy," but it is much deeper than that. . . . The Greek term translated "blessed" was used to describe two different conditions. First, it was used to describe the . . . wealthy who, by virtue of their riches, lived above the normal cares and worries of lesser folk. Second, the term was also used to describe the condition of the Greek gods who, because they had whatever they desired, existed in an unbelievable state of well-being, satisfaction, and contentment.

By repeating the same word to His band of simple-hearted, loyal followers, [Jesus] reassured them that enviable qualities such as delight, contentment, fulfillment, and . . . joy were theirs to claim. . . . He promised that by tossing aside all the extra baggage that accompanies religious hypocrisy and a performance-oriented lifestyle, we will travel the road that leads to inner peace. In doing so, we become "blessed."

Simple Faith

Aren't you glad that it is purity and not performance that brings blessing? What would a blessed life look like for you?

_____

_____

_____

DO THE GOOD YOU CAN

*Do not withhold good from those who deserve it
when it's in your power to help them.*
PROVERBS 3:27

Matthew Henry wrote: "Wherever the Providence of God casts us, we should desire and endeavor to be useful; and, when we cannot do the good we would, we must be ready to do the good we can. And he that is faithful in a little shall be entrusted with more."

That thought moves me. If you can't do the good you *would*, do the good you *can*. You may have had big-time plans in your life—Major League dreams that haven't panned out. You were going to write a best-selling book, but the opportunities just haven't come along. Are you willing to write for your church newsletter?

Maybe you wanted to teach in seminary or Bible school, but the pressures of life forced you in a different direction. Are you willing to teach a Sunday school class? . . . Maybe you'd hoped to be a missionary . . . but for one reason or another, that door has never opened. . . . Are you open to working with immigrants or refugees in your own city?

Moses: A Man of Selfless Dedication

Have you been striving to do great things and failing to do good things? What good can you do right where God has you?

_____

_____

GOD IS IN CONTROL

*Don't be impressed with your own wisdom. Instead,
fear the LORD and turn away from evil.*
PROVERBS 3:7

What often looks as if it is here to stay . . . can be frighteningly temporary. When God says, "That's it; that's curtains," it's only a matter of time. It is the perspective in all of this that holds us together. Our God is in complete control. He lets nothing out of His grip.

Yet our Lord is not some tyrannical god who stomps across heaven like the giant in *Jack in the Beanstalk,* swinging a club and waiting to give us a smashing blow to the head. No. Rather it is as if He says to us, "You're Mine, and I want you to walk in step with Me. I've arranged a plan so that walking with Me will result in a righteous lifestyle. If you make a decision not to walk with Me, I've also arranged consequences that will happen, and you must live with them."

Yes, life is short. Yes, our sins are obvious. . . . But instead of thinking of these days as just about as futile as emptying wastebaskets, see the significance of them in light of God's plan. . . . He has a way of balancing out the good with the bad.

Living Above the Level of Mediocrity

Do you find freedom in knowing that God is in control? That all you must do is follow in His steps?

_____

_____

OUR JOB IS TO OBEY

But let all who take refuge in you rejoice; let them sing joyful praises forever.
PSALM 5:11

As you walk the path of trust you will experience situations that simply defy explanation. When you look back, after the fact, you could never have figured out a better plan. At the time it seemed strange, mysterious . . . even illogical. Let me assure you, that's God working. Things will happen that seem to be totally contradictory, but these are God's arrangements. It was a wonderful day when I finally realized I don't have to explain or defend the will of God. My job is simply to obey it.

It is a waste of time trying to unscrew the inscrutable workings of God. You'll never be able to do it. That's simply the way God works. He honors faith and obedience. He will honor your faith if you will trust Him in a walk of obedience. And when you trust Him completely, you will enjoy inner quietness and security. You will have a secure confidence that you are walking in His will. You will be surrounded by His peace.

Perfect Trust

Have you caused yourself stress trying to understand the ways of God? What if you accepted that some things are not yours to know?

_____

_____

_____

A STOREHOUSE OF PROMISES

There was God's promise . . . saying: "I will certainly bless you,
and I will multiply your descendants beyond number."
HEBREWS 6:13–14

God's Book is a veritable storehouse of promises—more than seven thousand of them. Not empty hopes and dreams, not just nice-sounding, eloquently worded thoughts that make you feel warm all over, but promises. Verbal guarantees in writing, signed by the Creator Himself, in which He declares He will do or will refrain from doing specific things.

In a world of liars, cheats, deceivers, and con artists, isn't it a relief to know there is Someone you can trust? If He said it, you can count on it. Unlike the rhetoric of politicians who promise anybody anything they want to hear to get elected, what God says, God does.

The Finishing Touch

Have you ever been let down by someone you thought you could trust? Isn't it a comfort to know that God is a promise keeper?

_____

_____

_____

_____

_____

AN UNSHAKABLE FOUNDATION

*Though a mighty army surrounds me, my heart will
not be afraid. . . . I will remain confident.*
PSALM 27:3

The Hebrew term used by David in this psalm and translated *confident* does not mean self-reliant nor brave, humanly speaking. In Hebrew it means "to trust, to be secure, to have assurance." Its Arabic counterpart is picturesque: "to throw oneself down upon one's face, to lie upon the ground." The point here is that the source of David's confidence and stability was not his own strength—but God. His Lord was his only foundation for rock-like stability. What an unshakable foundation!

When pressure mounts, when a groundswell of fear invites panic, to whom do you turn?

Living Beyond the Daily Grind

What enemies or challenges are you facing today? Are you trusting the unshakable foundation of the Lord?

_____

_____

_____

_____

_____

YOU ARE GOD'S PERSONAL CONCERN

When people's lives please the LORD, even their enemies are at peace with them.

PROVERBS 16:7

You know what? God personally cares about the things that worry us. He cares more about them than we care about them: those things that hang in our minds as nagging, aching, worrisome thoughts.

Moses had some worrisome thoughts dragging him down. Do you remember why he left Egypt . . . ? He was running for his life. Pharaoh and some of his men were looking for Moses, to kill him (Exodus 2:15). Then forty years later God told Moses to return to Egypt (Exodus 3 and 4). Naturally Moses was worried about those men back in Egypt who wanted his head. He was reluctant to go back. But once he acquiesced to God's will, he said, "Lord, I'm available. I'm going to trust in You with all my heart. I'm not going to lean on my own understanding." Then while he was still in Midian, God said to him, "Oh, by the way, Moses, you know all the men who sought your life? They're dead." Isn't that remarkable? What a tremendous relief!

Perfect Trust

Is God calling you to something scary? Do you trust that He cares for you and knows how to take care of you?

_____

_____

_____

ALL WALLS FINALLY FALL

For Christ himself has brought peace to us. . . . He broke
down the wall of hostility that separated us.
EPHESIANS 2:14

All walls fall . . . eventually. No matter how well-constructed or long-standing it is, the wall will fall. It may be as intimidating as an angry giant or as silent as thin air and just as invisible, like the stubborn will of a person or the bitter spirit of an individual. But all walls finally fall.

Anyone who knows even a little history knows how true that is. To this day, archaeologists' spades continue to unearth the fallen walls of the world's great empires. Egyptian walls. Grecian walls. Roman walls. French walls. German walls. Russian walls.

All walls finally fall. Even our own. Even those built up against us. In the final analysis, Christ conquers! . . . There is no wall so great but that He is not greater still.

Esther: A Woman of Strength and Dignity

Can you even fathom the wall that separated you from God and the greatness of God's love that was able to remove it?

_____

_____

_____

AN ATTITUDE OF SATISFACTION

Don't wear yourself out trying to get rich. Be wise enough to know when to quit.

PROVERBS 23:4

To the surprise of many people, the Bible says a great deal about money. It talks about earning and spending, saving and giving, investing and even wasting our money. But in none of this does it ever come near to suggesting that money brings ultimate security.

If there were one great message I could deliver to those who struggle with not having an abundance of this world's good, it would be this simple yet profound premise for happiness. For a moment, let's go at it backward, from right to left.

That which constitutes great wealth is not related to money. It is an attitude of satisfaction ("enough is enough") coupled with inner peace (an absence of churning) plus a day-by-day, moment-by-moment walk with God. Sounds so simple, so right, so good, doesn't it? In our world of more, more, more . . . push, push, push . . . grab, grab, grab, this counsel is long overdue. In a word, the secret is *contentment*.

Strengthening Your Grip

Are you rich in the things that matter? How could you more effectively pursue contentment and intimacy with Christ?

_____

_____

HOPE REVIVED

For I am waiting for you, O LORD. You must answer for me, O Lord my God.
PSALM 38:15

Take from us our wealth and we are hindered. Take our health and we are handicapped. Take our purpose and we are slowed, temporarily confused. But take away our hope, and we are plunged into deepest darkness . . . stopped dead in our tracks, paralyzed. Wondering, "Why?" Asking, "How much longer? Will this darkness ever end? Does He know where I am?"

Then the Father says, "That's far enough," and how sweet it is! Like blossoms in the snow, long-awaited color returns to our life. The stream, once frozen, starts to thaw. Hope revives and washes over us.

Inevitably, spring follows winter. Every year. Yes, including this one.

The Finishing Touch

How has hope enabled you to endure the harsh circumstances of life? What promises do you cling to in hard times?

_____

_____

_____

_____

_____

THE URGENCY OF THE HOUR

*"I am coming soon. Hold on to what you have, so
that no one will take away your crown."*

REVELATION 3:11

If you live in the light of Christ's return each day of your life, it does wonders for your perspective. If you realize that you must give account for every idle word and action when you stand before the Lord Jesus, it does amazing things to your conduct. It also makes you recognize how many needless activities we get involved in on this earth. Sort of like rearranging the deck chairs on the *Titanic*. Don't bother! Don't get lost in insignificant details! He's coming soon! Recognize the urgency and the simplicity of the hour!

Hope Again

How would you live, speak, and treat others if you knew that today was the day of Christ's return?

Pleasure and Pain

I trust in you, my God! Do not let me be disgraced,
or let my enemies rejoice in my defeat.
Psalm 25:2

It's impossible to pass through life without experiencing times when you cannot see your way through a deep valley. Times when the package delivered at the back door comes delivered in the ugly wrapping of death or affliction or illness or even divorce. . . . John Selden, the old British jurist and scholar, put it even more bluntly. "Pleasure is nothing else but the intermission of pain."

You may find yourself enjoying the intermission. Today, you may be smiling. Your heart may be light and merry. Perhaps answers to prayer have come beautifully and deliberately. You are swept away in delight. But it's also quite possible that you are caught in the grip of affliction. You may be going through some of the hardest days of your life. You may be wondering, *Why? Why me? Why this trial?*

When you persevere through a trial, God gives you a special measure of insight. You become the recipient of the favor of God as He gives to you something that would not be learned otherwise.

Perfect Trust

Have your greatest lessons come through times of pleasure or times of pain? Why do you think this is so?

_____

_____

LOOK HEAVENWARD

For the LORD sees clearly what a man does, examining every path he takes.
PROVERBS 5:21

God is exacting in His knowledge. . . . Not one detail escapes His attention. . . . He knows everything about us. We are an open book before Him. Furthermore, He is immutably faithful. And yet He deliberately surprises us with difficult assignments, premature or unexpected deaths, lost jobs, and disappointing circumstances along the journey, even while we're in the nucleus of His will. Let's face it. It's a mystery.

Wherever you are in this journey called life, wherever you may be employed, wherever you may be in your domestic situation, wherever you may be in your age, your health, or your lifestyle, God may be preparing you for a great surprise in order to find you faithful. Rather than running from Him, let me suggest the opposite: run *toward* Him. . . . Look heavenward and realize that this arrangement is sovereignly put together for your good and for His glory.

The Mystery of God's Will

What if you viewed today's trials as opportunities to be found faithful? How can you draw closer to God in the midst of them?

_____

_____

_____

TENDER AND TOLERANT

Wisdom flows from the wise like a bubbling brook.
PROVERBS 18:4

George Washington Carver said, "How far you go in life depends on your being tender with the young, compassionate with the aged, sympathetic with the striving, and tolerant of the weak and the strong. Because someday in life you will have been all of these."

I have admired those words for years. They reflect a perspective easily forgotten in a dizzy schedule of demands and deadlines. It is easy in such a scene to become shortsighted, to think that now is forever. But those who sustain a close companionship with wisdom tend to be more tender, compassionate, sympathetic, and tolerant than those whose world revolves around themselves.

With wisdom comes depth and stability. When we navigate through life under full sail with wisdom at the helm, we may not miss all of the storms, but we will have the strength to persevere. We can face the unforeseen without the fear of sinking.

Growing Wise in Family Life

How have your life experiences given you more patience with others who struggle and more perseverance in the midst of your own struggles?

_____

_____

_____

A LIGHT FOR THE PATH

Your word is a lamp to guide my feet and a light for my path.

PSALM 119:105

A healthy fear of God will do much to deter us from sin. When we have a proper fear of the living Lord, we live a cleaner life. Any born-again person who sins willfully has momentarily blocked out his fear of God. You and I can do that. When we actively engage in sin, we consciously put aside what we know to be the truth about God. We suppress the knowledge of Him in our hearts and minds. We lie to ourselves by saying, "We'll get by. God won't mind so much."

I must say that this wholesome fear of the Almighty has turned up missing in our era. And when it is absent, we think we may do as we please. You can live as you please if you know you're not being seen and you won't get caught. But if, down deep inside, you know there is a living and holy God who will not let you get away with sin, you will avoid sin at all costs.

Moses: A Man of Selfless Dedication

When have you been tempted to stray from God's will, but the conviction of the Spirit kept you on the right path?

_____

_____

_____

_____

CHOOSE YOUR ATTITUDE

Those who trust their own insight are foolish, but
anyone who walks in wisdom is safe.
PROVERBS 28:26

This may shock you, but I believe the single most significant decision I can make on a day-to-day basis is my choice of attitude. It is more important than my past, my education, my bankroll, my successes or failures, fame or pain, what other people think of me or say about me, my circumstances, or my position. Attitude . . . keeps me going or cripples my progress. It alone fuels my fire or assaults my hope. When my attitudes are right, there's no barrier too high, no valley too deep, no dream too extreme, no challenge too great for me.

Yet, we must admit that we spend more of our time concentrating and fretting over the things that can't be changed in life than we do giving attention to the one thing that can, our choice of attitude.

Strengthening Your Grip

Do you allow the day-to-day cares of life to determine your attitude, or do you choose the peace and joy that is yours in Christ?

_____

_____

_____

_____

AUGUST

YOU LOST—GET OVER IT

Accept each other just as Christ has accepted you so that God will be given glory.
ROMANS 15:7

If you don't get your way, get over it, get on with life. If you don't get your way in a vote at a church, get over it. The vote was taken (if the church has integrity, the vote was handled with fairness); now get on with it. Just press on. And don't rehearse the fight or the vote year after year. The work of God slows down when we are not big enough to take it on the chin and say, "We lost!" Having been raised in the South, I didn't know the South lost the Civil War until I was in junior high school . . . and even then it was debatable among my teachers.

Be big enough to say, "We lost." Grace will help.

The Grace Awakening

Have you been a sore loser in your life? Is there something that you need to let go of and get over?

_____

_____

_____

_____

_____

SHARED JOY IS DOUBLE JOY

Two people are better off than one, for they can help each other succeed.
ECCLESIASTES 4:9

There's an old Swedish motto that hangs in many a kitchen: "Shared joy is a double joy. Shared sorrow is half a sorrow." . . . The secret of survival is not simply enjoying life's joys and enduring its sorrows; it is in sharing both with others.

We gain perspective by having somebody at our side. We gain objectivity. We gain courage in threatening situations. Having others near tempers our dogmatism and softens our intolerance. We gain another opinion. We gain what today, in our technical world, is called "input."

In other words, it is better not to work or live one's life all alone. It's better not to minister all alone. It's better to have someone alongside us in the battle. For that reason, during my days in the marines, we were taught that if the command "dig in" were issued, we should dig a hole large enough for two.

Living on the Ragged Edge

In a society that sometimes promotes individualism and isolation, what are you doing to maintain fellowship with other believers?

_____

_____

_____

GOD NEVER LEADS US ASTRAY

Lead me in the right path, O LORD. . . . Make your way plain for me to follow.
PSALM 5:8

God's voice isn't all that difficult to hear. In fact, you almost have to be closing your eyes and stopping your ears to miss it. He sometimes shouts through our pain, whispers to us while we're relaxing on vacation, occasionally He sings to us in a song, and warns us through the sixty-six books of His written Word. It's right there, ink on paper. Count on it—that book will never lead you astray.

In addition to His unfailing source of wisdom, He has given you wise counselors, friends, acquaintances, parents, teachers, and mentors who have earned your love and respect through long years. Screen what you believe to be the will of God through their thoughts, their perspectives. Does your conviction about the direction you're headed grow, or are you seeing lots of red flags and caution signs? Before you undertake a major life-direction change, be very careful that it is God's voice, that it is God's call you are hearing.

Moses: A Man of Selfless Dedication

Have you recently wondered why God isn't speaking in a certain situation? Could it be that you simply don't like what He is saying?

_____

_____

_____

KNOWING YOUR CHILD

*Direct your children onto the right path, and when
they are older, they will not leave it.*

PROVERBS 22:6

When it comes to rearing children, developing a strong home where happiness and harmony can flourish, there is a primary starting point: *knowing* your child. This is the most profound insight, the single most helpful secret I can pass on to you on the subject of child-rearing.

Do not think that just because you have conceived, carried, and finally given birth to your little one, you automatically know your child. Nor can you say you know him or her just because you live in the same house. I must say, categorically, *you do not*. Knowing your child takes time, careful observation, diligent study, prayer, concentration, help from above, and, yes, wisdom. Notice I did not include in that list a high IQ or some course in school. The two essential ingredients are desire and time. If you really want to know, and if you're willing to invest the time, God will honor your efforts. He will enable you to know your child.

Growing Wise in Family Life

Does your current schedule of activities allow time for simply getting to know your child? Does conversation need to replace entertainment?

_____

_____

A PLACE FOR PRAYER

Therefore, let all the godly pray to you.
PSALM 32:6

Never underestimate the place of prayer. . . . I'm convinced that one of the reasons we are so lax in prayer is that we have never prepared a place to meet with God. When you want to draw near to the heart of God, you have to get away from the din, away from the confusion, away from the noise and distractions. . . . You need a place apart—a place where you can separate yourself from the distractions of daily life and meet, alone, with God.

Then, be specific in your prayer life. If you need a job, pray for a job. If you're an engineer, ask God to open up an engineering position for you, or something related for which you are qualified. . . . If you need fifteen hundred dollars for tuition, ask for that amount. If some fear has you in its grasp, name that fear and ask specifically for relief from it. . . . "We need," as one of my mentors used to say, "to guard against the slimy ooze of indefiniteness."

Make your petitions specific.

Elijah: A Man of Heroism & Humility

Are you guilty of generic, half-hearted prayers? What specific need do you need to bring to the Lord today?

_____

_____

_____

JOY THROUGHOUT OUR DAYS

When people live to be very old, let them rejoice in every day of life.
ECCLESIASTES 11:8

Happiness is for today. Joy is available now. We are not to put it on hold. Happiness isn't something that will secretly open up to us when we turn fifty-five, or when we reach some goal or find the right marriage partner. Happiness is for *now*. It is inseparably linked to the living Lord.

A catechism in the Presbyterian church begins with the question, "What is the chief end of man?" The answer to that question is familiar to many: "The chief end of man is to love God and enjoy Him forever." Not just serve Him, not just obey Him, not just sacrifice to Him, not simply commit ourselves to Him, but enjoy Him—"Laugh through life with Him." Smile in His presence. So much more is included in enjoying Him forever than most would ever believe.

Happiness is to pervade all the years of our life. We don't have to wait until we reach some magical age when we are allowed to crack open the door and slip silently into the realm of happiness. It's there for us to enjoy *throughout* our days.

Living on the Ragged Edge

Are you presently enjoying God? Why might you be putting your happiness on hold?

_____

_____

_____

SELFISH DESIRES OR GOD'S DESIRES?

Fire tests the purity of silver and gold, but the LORD tests the heart.
PROVERBS 17:3

Ask yourself three questions of discipleship:
As you think through the major decisions you have recently made (during the past six to eight months), have they pleased the Lord or fed your ego?

Have you begun to take your personal goals and desires before the Lord or fed your ego?

Are you really willing to change those goals if, while praying about them, the Lord should lead you to do so?

Discipleship refuses to let us skate through life tossing around a few religious comments while we live as we please. It says, "There can be no more important relationship to you than the one you have with Jesus Christ." And it also says, "When you set forth your goals and desires in life, say no to the things that will only stroke your ego, and yes to the things that will deepen your commitment to Christ."

Strengthening Your Grip

Can you think of a time when, after praying it through, the Lord changed your heart on a matter?

_____

_____

_____

MERCY BEYOND MISERY

He shows mercy from generation to generation to all who fear him.

LUKE 1:50

I have a dear friend who stayed by his wife's side for almost a year as she was dying with ovarian cancer. He told me of such occasions, when the Lord gave merciful relief from the pain. He said it was almost as if an angel of mercy hovered over their room.

When we're suffering the consequences of unfair treatment, there is mercy with God. When we're enduring the grief of loss, there is mercy. When we struggle with the limitations of a handicap, there is mercy. When we're hurting and in physical pain, there is mercy. All these earthly struggles that occur are no accident. God is in the midst of them, working out His sovereign will. Yes, it's a mystery, which means we need special mercy to endure the anguish and misery of the pain.

The Mystery of God's Will

When has the mercy of the Lord enabled you to endure earthly pain and loss?

_____

_____

_____

_____

233

DEVELOPING INWARD BEAUTY

*Charm is deceptive, and beauty does not last; but a woman
who fears the LORD will be greatly praised.*
PROVERBS 31:30

External beauty is ephemeral. Internal beauty is eternal. The former is
attractive to the world; the latter is pleasing to God. Peter describes this
inner beauty as "a gentle and quiet spirit" (1 Peter 3:4). This might be para-
phrased "a gentle tranquility." Without question, this is any woman's most
powerful quality—true character. And such character comes from within—from
the hidden person of the heart—because you know who you are and you know
whom you adore and serve, the Lord Christ.

Outward adornment doesn't take a great deal of time. I've seen women do it
in a few minutes on their way to work in the morning. . . . But it takes a lifetime
to prepare and develop the hidden person of the heart.

Hope Again

In a world that celebrates external beauty, how are you cultivating an
inner beauty that pleases the Lord?

THE IMAGE OF GOD'S SON

And the Lord—who is the Spirit—makes us more and more
like him as we are changed into his glorious image.

2 CORINTHIANS 3:18

Maybe you've never before stopped to consider that God is committed to one major objective in the lives of all His people: to conform us to the "image" of His Son. We need to blow the dust off that timeless goal now that our cage is overcrowded and our lives are growing increasingly more distant from each other.

Exactly what does our heavenly Father want to develop within us? What is that "image" of His Son? I believe the simple answer is found in Christ's own words. Listen as He declares His primary reason for coming: "For even the Son of Man did not come to be served, but to serve, and to give His life as a ransom for many" (Mark 10:45 NASB).

No mumbo jumbo. Just a straight-from-the-shoulder admission. He came to serve and to give. It makes sense, then, to say that God desires the same for us.

Dropping Your Guard

How much of your time and resources are devoted to serving others instead of self? Are your activities making you more like Christ?

_____

_____

_____

A PERFECT PLAN

He said, "It is finished!" Then he bowed his head and gave up his spirit.
JOHN 19:30

Though unbelieving men nailed Jesus to His cross, it occurred "by the predetermined plan and foreknowledge of God" (Acts 2:23 NASB). It was exactly at the time and in the place and by the means God had determined. And what looked to the eleven confused disciples as mysterious, as well as unfair and unjust (humanly speaking, it was all of the above and more), God looked at it and said, "That is what I've planned. That's the mission My Son came to accomplish."

That's why Jesus' final words from the cross before He died were "It is finished." God's redemption plan had been completed—Jesus' payment for our sin. And then He slumped in death.

The Mystery of God's Will

What does it mean for your life that Christ accomplished what He came to do? That there is no stopping the perfect plan of God?

_____

_____

_____

_____

SAILS SET TOWARD JOY

A glad heart makes a happy face.
PROVERBS 15:13

I have discovered that a joyful countenance has nothing to do with one's age or one's occupation (or lack of it) or one's geography or education or marital status or good looks or circumstances. . . . Joy is a choice. It is a matter of attitude that stems from one's confidence in God—that He is at work, that He is in full control, that He is in the midst of whatever has happened, is happening, and will happen. Either we fix our minds on that and determine to laugh again, or we wail and whine our way through life, complaining that we never got a fair shake. We are the ones who consciously determine which way we shall go.

Regardless how severely the winds of adversity may blow, we set our sails toward joy.

Laugh Again

Have you experienced joy in the most unlikely of times? What does this tell you about the nature of joy?

_____

_____

_____

_____

237

THE WILL TO DO GOD'S WILL

"Our Father in heaven, may your name be kept holy."
MATTHEW 6:9

By merely reviewing the first few lines of the Lord's Prayer, we gain a renewed respect . . . a healthy and wholesome sense of reverence for our almighty God and Father. Rather than causing us to run from Him and hide in fear, I find that such an awesome respect makes me want to come close to Him, to wait quietly for Him to work. And so I urge you to slow your pace, to approach His "hallowed name" thoughtfully. Take time! Give Him the respect He deserves. Wait on God. In return, He will give you a clearer vision. Furthermore, He will soften your will and make you want to know and do His will.

Simple Faith

How much time do you set aside for prayer each day? What other activities can you shorten or remove to give more time to sitting in God's presence?

_____

_____

_____

_____

_____

SENSITIVE HEARTS

For the kind of sorrow God wants us to experience leads us away from
sin and results in salvation. There's no regret for that kind of sorrow.

2 CORINTHIANS 7:10

C an you name people today who seem to listen carefully to God—people whose hearts are especially sensitive to the Holy Spirit? I can almost guarantee that those are men and women who know what it is to be broken and bruised. They have the scars to prove it.

Perhaps as you read these words you bear the marks of a worldly week, day after day in which you've gone your own way and grieved the Spirit of God. And now you come to these pages with desperation to change in your heart—to learn from God and renew your fellowship with Him. Do you realize what's happened? Your failure has given you a sensitive, teachable spirit. It has broken the pride barrier in your life. It is what Paul called a "godly sorrow" (2 Corinthians 7:10 NKJV).

Moses: A Man of Selfless Dedication

How do you know if it's conviction or condemnation? Is it driving you toward God or away? Godly sorrow draws you closer.

_____

_____

_____

GIVE ALL YOU HAVE

Fear of the LORD is the foundation of wisdom. Knowledge of the Holy One results in good judgment.
PROVERBS 9:10

If you're the kind of Christian who really wants the whole purpose of God, then you dare not leave out kingdom commitment. That means your motives must be investigated. For example, every time you make plans to acquire a sizable possession—a car, an expensive boat, a house, and such like—you must deal with it before God and ask: Is this His will? Would this honor Him? Would this glorify Him?

Am I suggesting that you take a vow of poverty? No, not that. My message is not that you go hungry and give up all nice things. I just say you give up *control* of them. Give all you have to the Lord God and trust Him to give back all that you need.

Living Above the Level of Mediocrity

Are your possessions serving God's purposes or your pleasure? Do you need to reevaluate the motives behind your purchases?

VISION, VITALITY, AND VICTORY

May integrity and honesty protect me, for I put my hope in you.
PSALM 25:21

Thoughts are the thermostat that regulates what we accomplish in life. My body responds and reacts to the input from my mind. If I feed my mind upon doubt, disbelief, and discouragement, that is precisely the kind of day my body will experience. If I adjust my thermostat forward to thoughts filled with vision, vitality, and victory, I can count on that kind of day.

Thoughts, positive or negative, grow stronger when fertilized with constant repetition. That may explain why so many who are gloomy and gray stay in that mood . . . and why those who are cheery and enthusiastic continue to be so.

You need only one foreman in your mental factory; Mr. Triumph is His name. He is anxious to assist you. . . . His real name is the Holy Spirit, the Helper.

The Finishing Touch

How do you regulate what goes into your mind? Are you constantly evaluating and separating garbage from gospel?

_____

_____

_____

_____

241

HEARTS TO TRUST, MINDS TO REST

Give your burdens to the LORD, and he will take care of
you. He will not permit the godly to slip and fall.
PSALM 55:22

God has entrusted to us a great deal. He knows that we can do all things by His grace, so He's trusting in us to trust in Him. Yet He knows our fears as well; otherwise He wouldn't assure us so often of His purposes and His presence.

We feel hurt and alone—God assures us He cares.

We feel angry and resentful—God provides wisdom and strength.

We feel ashamed—God grants forgiveness and comfort.

We feel anxious—God promises to supply all our needs.

May He give us ears to hear, hearts to trust, and minds to rest in Him. Our God is uniquely and ultimately trustworthy!

Perfect Trust

What burden do you need to turn over to the Lord? Do you trust Him to carry it for you?

_____

_____

_____

_____

SLOW BUT SURE

You can be sure of this: The LORD set apart the godly for himself. The LORD will answer when I call to him.

PSALM 4:3

Where are you today on your own journey? Are you discounting the significance of your days? Are you sighing rather than singing? Are you wondering what good can come from all that you have to live with?

We tend to think that if God is really engaged, He will change things within the next hour or so. Certainly by sundown. Absolutely by the end of the week. But God is not a slave to the human clock. Compared to the works of mankind, He is extremely deliberate and painfully slow. As religious poet George Herbert wisely penned, "God's mill grinds slow, but sure."

God's hand is not so short that it cannot save, nor is His ear so heavy that He cannot hear. Whether you see Him or not, He is at work in your life this very moment. God specializes in turning the mundane into the meaningful. . . . One of my longtime friends, Howie Stevenson, often says with a smile, "God moves among the casseroles."

Esther: A Woman of Strength and Dignity

What have you been praying about for years? God is always at work behind the scenes.

_____

_____

PRAISE AND ADORATION

Your unfailing love is better than life itself; how I praise you!
PSALM 63:3

P raise is a deeply significant aspect of our personal worship, and we are remiss if we ignore it. . . . We *praise* God by expressing words of honor to Him for His character, His name, His will, His Word, His glory, etc.

Husband, when you were dating your wife-to-be, can you remember doing this? You looked at her hair . . . and you expressed praise over her hair. You praised her for her beauty, her choice of perfume and clothing, and her excellent taste. . . . Praise came naturally because that was a genuine, stimulating part of romance. By the way, I hope you haven't *stopped* praising her! Praise is greatly appreciated by your wife, and likewise by our Lord.

Praise is to flow from within us. Praise is an aspect of prayer—adoration directed to God.

Living Beyond the Daily Grind

How much of your prayer time is spent simply praising? Take a moment and simply adore the Lord.

_____

_____

_____

_____

WE NEED EACH OTHER

Yes, there are many parts, but only one body.
1 CORINTHIANS 12:20

Nobody is a whole chain. Each one is a link. But take away one link and the chain is broken.

Nobody is a whole team. Each one is a player. But take away one player and the game is forfeited.

Nobody is a whole orchestra. Each one is a musician. But take away one musician and the symphony is incomplete.

You guessed it. We need each other. You need someone and someone needs you. Isolated islands we're not.

To make this thing called life work, we gotta lean and support. And relate and respond. And give and take. And confess and forgive. And reach out and embrace.

The Finishing Touch

Who in your life makes you more like Christ? How does fellowship with other believers make your life richer?

_____

_____

_____

_____

SOLID AS STONE

For God bought you with a high price. So you must honor God with your body.
1 CORINTHIANS 6:20

Committed individuals live with shallow tent pegs. They may own things, but nothing owns them. They have come to terms with merchandise that has a price tag and opted for commitment to values that are priceless.

Denying oneself is not to be equated with losing one's uniqueness or becoming of no value. There have been great people in each generation who modeled self-denial as they made significant contributions to humankind.

For years I taught that we are to "count the cost." It seemed so plausible. But suddenly one day, it dawned on me that Jesus never once told His followers to count the cost. No—He's the One who has already done that. He is the King who has already determined what it will take to encounter and triumph over life's enemies. And what will it take? A few strong, quality-minded champions whose commitment is solid as stone.

Living Above the Level of Mediocrity

Have you learned to hold loosely the things of this world? What do you consider most valuable in your life?

_____

_____

_____

Is the Motive Right?

Better to have little, with fear for the Lord, than to have great treasure and inner turmoil.

PROVERBS 15:16

Fortune says that to be successful you need to make the big bucks. Why else would the Fortune 500 list make such headlines every year? Anyone who is held up as successful must have more money than the average person.

Understand, there is nothing wrong with money earned honestly. Certainly there is nothing wrong in investing or giving or even spending money if the motive is right, if the heart is pure. But I have yet to discover anyone who has found true happiness simply in the gathering of more money. Although money is not sinful or suspect in itself, it is not what brings lasting contentment, fulfillment, or satisfaction.

Hope Again

Do you know someone who is wealthy and unsatisfied? Poor and content? Does it change the way you view earthly riches?

_____

_____

_____

_____

A STRING OF MOMENTS

*Keep your servant from deliberate sins! Don't let them control
me. Then I will be free of guilt and innocent of great sin.*
PSALM 19:13

L ife on earth is really nothing more than a string of moments, one after
another. And I do not want my testimony for Jesus Christ to be shattered by
a single moment of indulging my flesh. I don't want *one moment* of rage or pride
or arrogance to cast a shadow over a lifetime of walking with my Lord. Frankly,
I fear that possibility. And do you know what? I *want* to fear that possibility.
When I stop fearing it, I am in grave danger.

The Living Bible renders David's prayer (Psalm 19:13): "Keep me from deliberate wrongs; help me to stop doing them. Only then can I be free of guilt and
innocent of some great crime."

What a great prayer! "Lord, You know my capacity to throw everything
over in one stupid, fleshly act. Keep me from it! Restrain me. Guard me from
trashing it all in one horrible moment of rage or lust. If You guard me and keep
me, Lord, I'll never have to look back and mourn over committing such a deed."

Moses: A Man of Selfless Dedication

Are you aware of your capacity for sin? How can you specifically pray for
the Lord to protect you from yourself?

_____

_____

GOD IS BIGGER THAN OUR EXCUSES

Then I heard the Lord asking, "Whom should I send as a
messenger to this people? Who will go for us?"

ISAIAH 6:8

We all have excuses to disqualify ourselves from God's service.
- "I'm not physically well."
- "I've got this temper problem."
- "I can't speak very well in public."
- "I don't have a lot of education."
- "My past is too raunchy!"
- "You see, I'm a divorcée."
- "I was once in a mental hospital."

And on and on and on. . . . But God is bigger than *any* of those reasons. He
specializes in taking bruised, soiled, broken, guilty, and miserable vessels and
making them whole, forgiven, and useful again.

You see, God's perspective is much broader than ours.

Strengthening Your Grip

Is there something about you or your past that you think disqualifies you
from God's service? It may be just the thing God uses.

_____

_____

_____

STOP RUNNING SCARED

I will be glad and rejoice in your unfailing love, for you have seen
my troubles, and you care about the anguish of my soul.
PSALM 31:7

Y ou may be going through a trial so overwhelming that it's borderline unbearable. You want to see the end of the tunnel. Which is only natural, because once we see that little speck of light, we feel we can make it through to the finish. But God's tunnels are often twisting, too complex and dark to see the light for many days. In such settings He says, "In that dark, twisting, seemingly endless period of time, trust Me. Stop running scared! Stop fearing!"

Perfect Trust

What darkness are you experiencing right now? Are you trusting in the promises of God?

_____

_____

_____

_____

_____

_____

PRAYER IS PRIVATE DEVOTION

"Pray to your Father in private. Then your Father,
who sees everything, will reward you."

MATTHEW 6:6

P rayer is never something we do to be seen. It loses its whole purpose if it becomes a platform to impress others. It is a private act of devotion, not a public demonstration of piety. According to Jesus, it belongs in the closet of our lives, an act done in secret.

Christ never saw a prayer as pleading or begging or hammering away at the throne of God. No, the Father knows His children, He knows what we need. Therefore, there is no reason to think that connecting with Him requires special words excessively repeated.

Prayer was never intended to be a verbal marathon for only the initiated . . . no secret-code talk for the clergy or a public display of piety. None of that. Real prayer—the kind of prayer Jesus mentioned and modeled—is realistic, spontaneous, down-to-earth communication with the living Lord that results in a relief of personal anxiety and a calm assurance that our God is in full control of our circumstances.

Strengthening Your Grip

Do you struggle with the right words when you pray? Could it be that you're making it more complicated than God intended?

_____

_____

A POSITION WE CAN'T FILL

So let's stop condemning each other.
ROMANS 14:13

E ach one of us belongs to the same Lord. When we stop dictating, it is easier for others to mature as they follow the Lord's directing.

Freeing others means we never assume a position we're not qualified to fill. This, in one sentence, is enough to stop any person from judging another. We're not qualified. We lack full knowledge. How often we have jumped to wrong conclusions, made judgmental statements, only to find out later how off base we were . . . then wished we could cut out our tongue? What keeps us from being qualified to judge?

We do not know all the facts.

We are unable to read motives.

We find it impossible to be totally objective.

We lack "the big picture."

We live with blind spots.

We are prejudiced and have blurred perspective.

Most of all, we ourselves are imperfect and inconsistent.

The Grace Awakening

Do you find yourself withholding grace from others and forgetting the massive amount of grace you have yourself received?

_____

A POSITIVE PERSPECTIVE

So I saw that there is nothing better for people than to
be happy in their work. That is our lot in life.
ECCLESIASTES 3:22

We usually can do very little to change our lot. We can only change our reaction to our lot. We cannot change our past, for example. I don't care how brilliant we are, our past stands in concrete. We cannot erase it. But we can learn today to see our past from God's perspective, and use the disadvantages of yesterday in our life—today and forever.

You and I constantly bump up against people submerged in self-pity. They are hopelessly lost in the swamp of life. And all they can tell you is how wrong this was, or how unfair she was, or how someone's promise was broken, or how that man walked away and left "me and the kids," or that guy broke up a partnership and "took me to the cleaners," and on and on and on.

But Solomon says, in effect, "I suggest to you that there's nothing better than that you look for an advantage and then dwell on it. Make that your life's message. Who knows what impact it will have?"

Living on the Ragged Edge

Do you find yourself focusing on past hurts and reliving them over and over? How can you redirect your thoughts instead?

_____

_____

_____

GOD'S WAYS DEFY EXPLANATION

Oh, how great are God's riches and wisdom and knowledge! How impossible it is for us to understand his decisions and his ways!
ROMANS 11:33

The New American Standard declares that last phrase: "*How ... unfathomable His ways!*" Maybe you've come to discover this in your own experience. You've tried to "trace out His path" and you can't pull it off. You've tried to fathom His "unfathomable" ways and you can't. It just doesn't compute. It blows your microprocessor. You have begun to walk with God like never before in your life, but in that path of obedience, you have come across situations that simply defy explanation—you have encountered situations that seem to be contradictory. That's how God works; accept it! It may not make sense to you for years, if ever. But that's okay. I've come to realize I wouldn't understand His thought processes and planned procedures, even if He took time to explain them to me.

It was a wonderful day for me when I finally realized I don't have to explain the will of God. That's not my task. My job is simply to obey it.

Moses: A Man of Selfless Dedication

What would happen if you decided to be okay not knowing what you weren't meant to know? What new freedoms would you experience?

_____

_____

_____

MOTHER'S INDELIBLE IMPRESSION

So give your father and mother joy! May she who gave you birth be happy.
PROVERBS 23:25

There is no more influential or powerful role on earth than a mother's. Significant as political, military, education, or religious public figures may be, none can compare to the impact made by mothers. Their words are never fully forgotten, their touch leaves an indelible impression, and the memory of their presence lasts a lifetime.

Abraham Lincoln was right: "No one is poor who had a godly mother." Instead of camping on the negatives and emphasizing how far many mothers have drifted from this magnificent calling to shape the future of our country, I want to throw out a positive challenge. Ladies, this is your hour . . . your distinct opportunity to soar! A harmonious marital partnership and a solid, unselfish commitment to motherhood have never been of greater importance to you or, for that matter, to our nation. Talk about a challenge worth your effort! In spite of what you may have heard, this role is the most dignified, the most influential, and the most rewarding in all the world.

Growing Wise in Family Life

Do you take pride in your role as wife and mother? Do you grasp the magnitude of your influence on your family?

_____

_____

GOD SUPPLIES REINFORCEMENTS

O Sovereign Lord, the strong one who rescued me,
you protected me on the day of battle.
PSALM 140:7

If you determine to live according to biblical standards, be sure that your enemy is seeking to devour you. You *will* encounter the darts of the devil. Someone put it this way: "Whoever desires to walk with God walks right into the crucible." All who choose godliness live in a crucible. The tests *will* come.

But all is not lost. Far from it! Our great hope and assurance is that the One in us is greater than the one in the world. We do not face such a formidable enemy that we cannot fight him or stand firm and secure in our decision. Our Lord is the God of hope. . . . His supply line never runs short. When His godly followers are in need, He is there to supply the necessary reinforcements. As you do battle, God will provide for all of your needs.

Moses: A Man of Selfless Dedication

As you strive to live a holy life, where does the enemy attack the most? Are you asking the Lord to guard you in that specific area?

_____

_____

_____

_____

SEPTEMBER

WE NEED DISCIPLINE

If you ignore criticism, you will end in poverty and disgrace;
if you accept correction, you will be honored.
PROVERBS 13:18

Discipline is one of the most hated terms of our times . . . right alongside *patience* and *self-control*. But have you noticed how often it comes up in the testimonies of those who win?

Here are some key uses of discipline:

No runner completes the training or a race without it.

No weight-loss program is maintained without it.

No human body is kept fit without it.

No mind is sharpened without it.

No temptation is overcome without it.

If you want to put a stop to mediocrity, to replace excuses with fresh determination and procrastination with tough-minded perseverance, you need discipline.

Day by Day with Charles Swindoll

Do you lack discipline in any area of your life? What practices can you put in place to improve in that area?

_____

_____

_____

THE RACE IS ON

I have observed something else under the sun. The fastest runner doesn't always win the race, and the strongest warrior doesn't always win the battle.

ECCLESIASTES 9:11

Whenever I scope out the scene here where I live, I observe a large number of people who are pursuing the so-called successful life. They would say the way to make it in this world—the way to succeed—is to increase speed, get stronger, be competitive, think more cleverly, plan longer, and have a visionary strategy—hire people with the skills that are needed, and life will be successful. The race is on. Get up earlier. Go to bed later. Make work a top priority. Don't get sentimental about stuff like children, marriage, home, and the family. All that will have to wait. . . . And religion? Leave that for the over-the-hill gang and preachers.

The philosophy of our day will attempt to suck us in and convince us that if we're going to make it, we've got to run faster. . . . We've got to be stronger and more competitive and more clever, even more manipulative. Otherwise, we won't be successful. . . . Don't you believe it!

Living on the Ragged Edge

Have you gotten caught up in the bigger is better, more is not enough mentality that this world promotes? How can you begin stepping back and slowing down today?

_____

_____

SALT AND LIGHT

"You are the salt of the earth.... You are the light of the world."
MATTHEW 5:13–14

God never promised us a rose garden. He came up front with us and admitted that the arena of this world is not a friend of grace to help us on to God. Nevertheless, strange as it may seem, He went on to tell a handful of Palestinian peasants (and *all* godly servants in *every* generation) that their influence would be nothing short of remarkable. They would be "the salt of the earth" and they would be "the light of the world." And so shall we! So far-reaching would be the influence of servants in society, their presence would be as significant as salt on food and as light on darkness. Neither is loud or externally impressive, but both are essential. Without our influence this old world would soon begin to realize our absence. Even though it may not admit it, society needs both salt and light.

Improving Your Serve

How are you being salt and light to the world around you? In your home, community, workplace?

_____

_____

_____

_____

_____

GOD'S GREAT FAITHFULNESS

The faithful love of the LORD never ends! His mercies never cease.

LAMENTATIONS 3:22

The Lord's mercies never cease.

The Lord's compassions never fail.

The Lord's faithfulness never diminishes.

That defines God's immutability, which means "He doesn't change." He never cools off in His commitment to us. He never breaks a promise or loses enthusiasm. He stays near us when we are jealous for the truth, and He stays near us when we reject His counsel and deliberately disobey.... His faithfulness is unconditional, unending, and unswerving. Nothing we do can diminish it, and nothing we stop doing can increase it.... Mysterious though such incredible constancy may seem, it's true.

The Mystery of God's Will

Have you ever experienced the betrayal or abandonment of a loved one? What does it mean for you to know that God is incapable of such a thing?

_____

_____

_____

_____

_____

ENDURANCE FINDS FAVOR WITH GOD

So if you are suffering in a manner that pleases God, keep on doing what is right, and trust your lives to the God who created you, for he will never fail you.
1 PETER 4:19

If you are a hard-working, faithful employee, diligent, honest, productive, prompt, caring, working for a boss who is belligerent, stubborn, short-sighted, and ungrateful, and if you patiently endure that situation—that finds favor with God. . . . When you endure, you put grace on display. And when you put grace on display for the glory of God, you could revolutionize your work-place or any other situation.

The purpose of the believer in society is to bring glory and honor to the name of Christ, not to be treated well or to have life be easy or even to be happy, as wonderful as all those things are.

Why are these things happening to you? So that you might follow in the steps of our Lord Jesus, who suffered for us.

Hope Again

When have you suffered for doing what is right? How does it feel knowing that such faithfulness pleases God?

_____

_____

_____

AN ENDLESS LITANY

Wise words bring many benefits, and hard work brings rewards.
PROVERBS 12:14

While we think we may be immune to the endless litany of television commercials, online ads, our friends' gadgets and gizmos, the constant admonition to spend, spend, spend, we Christians need to be alert to how Satan tempts us with the temporal. I'll mention a few ways to avoid the magnetism of the cash register or the credit card.

Doctrinal danger . . . substituting the temporal for the eternal.

Personal danger . . . trying to impress instead of imparting the Word.

Economical danger . . . spending more than you have.

Psychological danger . . . believing your purchase will make things "all right."

Make Hebrews 12:3 your aim: "Consider Him . . . so that you will not grow weary and lose heart" (NASB).

Day by Day with Charles Swindoll

Have you ever taken the easy way and suffered the consequences? Did you wish you had simply done the work required?

_____

_____

_____

_____

NOT ONE LOST MOMENT

So be careful how you live. Don't live like fools, but like those who are wise.
EPHESIANS 5:15

God tells us not to be foolish, but wise, making the most of our time, taking every opportunity that comes our way and using it wisely.

Before his twentieth birthday, Jonathan Edwards, the brilliant and godly philosopher-theologian who became God's instrument in the Great Awakening revival of the eighteenth century, resolved "never to lose one moment of time, but to improve it in the most profitable way I possibly can." That is exactly what he did, using well the intellectual gifts God had given him. He entered Yale at thirteen and at seventeen graduated at the head of his class. At twenty-six he was the minister of one of the largest congregations in Massachusetts.

Following the will of God requires wisdom, clear thinking, and, yes, even good old garden-variety common sense.

The Mystery of God's Will

Are you spending your days wisely and making each moment count for the glory of God?

_____

_____

_____

_____

THE DIFFERENCE MAKES THE DIFFERENCE

"Your love for one another will prove to the world that you are my disciples."
JOHN 13:35

If our message is a mirror image of the message of the world, the world yawns and goes on its way, saying, "What else is new? I've heard all that since I was born." But if the Christian lifestyle and motivation and answers are different, the world cannot help but sit up and take notice, thinking:

How is it that I cannot conquer this habit, but he has?

Why is their love so deep and lasting and ours so shallow and fickle?

How is it that she can forgive and never hold a grudge, but I can't get over a wrong?

Talk about kindness and courtesy! These people exude those things. I wonder why.

I've never seen such integrity. The guy wouldn't think of taking a dime that isn't his.

Do you get the message? It is the difference that makes the difference.

Simple Faith

Do you live in such a way that makes others stop and take notice? How are you living differently than those around you?

_____

_____

_____

SOLITUDE AND SERENITY

Tune your ears to wisdom, and concentrate on understanding.
PROVERBS 2:2

An inner restlessness grows within us when we refuse to get alone with God and examine our own hearts, including our motives. As our lives begin to pick up the debris that accompanies a lot of activities and involvements, we can train ourselves to go right on, to stay active, to be busy in the Lord's work. Unless we discipline ourselves to pull back, to get alone for the hard work of self-examination in times of solitude, serenity will remain only a distant dream. How busy we can become . . . and as a result, how empty! We mouth words, but they mean nothing. We find ourselves trafficking in unlived truths. We fake spirituality.

How easy to fall prey to meaningless talk, cliché-ridden responses, and mindless activities! It was never meant to be that way; but, more often than not, that's the way it is. To break the habit, solitude is required. The hard work of self-examination on a recurring basis is absolutely essential.

Intimacy with the Almighty

Have you ever found yourself busy doing "good things" and, yet, stressed and unsatisfied? Do you regularly reevaluate your activities to ensure they are what God desires?

_____

_____

HAPPILY EVER AFTER?

My suffering was good for me, for it taught me to pay attention to your decrees.
PSALM 119:71

H appily ever after" belongs at the end of a fairy tale, not in a description of the Christian life. Life in Christ is real. It isn't plastic, it isn't stained-glass, it isn't saccharine, it isn't fantasyland. In all my years of walking with the Lord, I have yet to meet one Christian who has "lived happily ever after." On the other hand, I have met a great many significant saints who have endured affliction, loss, disappointment, setbacks, failures, and incredible pain through the years. And I have seen many of those same men, women, and . . . adolescents cling to their joy, radiate hope, and sustain a winsome spirit . . . even through heartache . . . even through tears . . . even at death's door.

If you're waiting for a seamless, blemish-free week, friend, you're going to wait in vain. There is no such thing. And until we learn how to derive lessons from seasons of failure and loss, we'll keep repeating those failures—digging ourselves into an ever-deeper hole—rather than moving on as we grow up.

Moses: A Man of Selfless Dedication

Were you surprised at the trials that accompany a godly life? Are you genuine with others when discussing a life of obedience?

_____

_____

_____

WHEN THE GOING GETS ROUGH

I walk in righteousness, in paths of justice.
PROVERBS 8:20

Vision is the ability to see God's presence, to perceive God's power, to focus on God's plan in spite of the obstacles.

When you have vision it affects your attitude. Your attitude is optimistic rather than pessimistic. Your attitude stays positive rather than negative. Not foolishly positive, as though in fantasy, for you are reading God into your circumstances. So when a situation comes that cuts your feet out from under you, you don't throw up your arms and panic. You don't give up. Instead, you say, "Lord, this is Your moment. This is where You take charge. You're in this."

This is nothing more than having a strong belief in the power of God; having confidence in others around you who are in similar battles with you; and, yes, having confidence in yourself, by the grace of God. Refusing to give in to temptation, cynicism, and doubt. . . . It's hanging tough when the going gets rough.

Living Above the Level of Mediocrity

When were you tempted to quit but instead chose to walk faithfully with your Father? What benefits came from that faithfulness?

_____

_____

_____

THE BOOK OF BOOKS

To acquire wisdom is to love yourself; people who
cherish understanding will prosper.
PROVERBS 19:8

There is something grand about old things that are still in good shape. Old furniture, rich with the patina of age and history, is far more intriguing than the uncomfortable, modern stuff.

The Bible is old also—ancient, in fact. Its timeless stories have for centuries shouted, "You can make it! Don't quit. . . . Don't give up!" Its truths, secure and solid as stone, say, "I'm still here, waiting to be claimed and applied." Whether it's a prophet's warning, a patriarch's prayer, a poet's psalm, or a preacher's challenging reminder, the Book of books lives on, offering us new vistas.

Though ancient, it has never lost its relevance. Though battered, no one has ever improved on its content. Though old, it never fails to offer something pure, something wise, something new.

The Finishing Touch

Do you cherish the ancient wisdom found in God's Word? How are its commands and promises still relevant today?

_____

_____

_____

SPIRITUAL FUEL

Come and listen to my counsel. I'll share my heart with you and make you wise.
PROVERBS 1:23

What fuel is to a car, the Holy Spirit is to the believer. He energizes us to stay the course. He motivates us in spite of the obstacles. He keeps us going when the road gets rough. It is the Spirit who comforts us in our distress, who calms us in times of calamity, who becomes our companion in loneliness and grief, who spurs our "intuition" into action, who fills our minds with discernment when we are uneasy about a certain decision. In short, He is our spiritual fuel. When we attempt to operate without Him or to use some substitute fuel, all systems grind to a halt.

Flying Closer to the Flame

Have you gone through periods when your prayer life waned and your study of Scripture suffered? How did this affect your ability to endure hardships?

_____

_____

_____

_____

_____

TRUST WITHOUT RESERVATION

See, God has come to save me. I will trust in him and not be
afraid. The LORD GOD is my strength and my song.
ISAIAH 12:2

Christianity is trusting Christ, not self. Most people are trying to reach God, find God, and please God through their own efforts. But perfect trust is resting all of one's weight on something else, not on self. It's like resting on crutches to hold you up when you twist an ankle. You lean on them as your strength. Proverbs 3:5–6 teaches us to "trust in the LORD with all your heart and do not lean on your own understanding. In all your ways acknowledge Him, and He will make your paths straight" (NASB).

In other words, strength comes from proper perspective. Elton Trueblood put it this way: "Faith is not belief without proof, but trust without reservation." Strength comes from choosing to fully trust, pray, and praise. Our circumstances may not change, but in the process we change.

Perfect Trust

Are you working hard to please God or trusting in the work Christ has already done?

_____

_____

_____

JUST THE RIGHT MESSAGE

Let me hear of your unfailing love each morning, for I am trusting you.
PSALM 143:8

L isten to me, victims of mistreatment. More importantly, please listen to God's truth. He has a hundred different messages to give you during a hundred different dungeon experiences. He knows just the right message at just the right time, and all it takes to receive it is a sensitive, obedient, trusting heart. Not one preoccupied with revenge or bitterness or hostility, but a heart that says, "Lord, God, help me now. Right at this moment. Deliver me from my own prison. Help me to see beyond the darkness, to see Your hand. As I am being crushed, remold me. Help me to see You in this."

Pray that prayer. Turn your trial into trust as you look to God to tenderly use that affliction, that dungeon, that abandonment for His purpose.

In the midst of all this, remember, God has not abandoned you. He has not forgotten you. He never left. He understands the heartache.

Joseph: A Man of Integrity and Forgiveness

What promises bring you the most comfort in times of trouble? When have you felt God's presence during a difficult time?

_____

_____

_____

AN EXTRAORDINARY DAY

"I will come to you suddenly, as unexpected as a thief."
REVELATION 3:3

Most of our days begin rather predictably. Day after day, for the most part, we could enter into our diary the same three words: "No big deal." Days don't begin with divine skywriting. . . . Angelic choirs don't waken us with celestial harmony, blending their voices in the "Hallelujah Chorus." . . . However, days that begin uneventfully can also lead into an unbelievable, indescribable series of heart-stopping experiences. Ordinary days, in fact, can become extraordinary.

How about the day Jesus arrived? There wasn't one citizen in Judea who awoke that morning expecting the day to bring such a life-changing event in the village of Bethlehem.

And what about the day . . . of Christ's return? . . . Homemakers will be shopping. Planes will be taking off and landing. . . . Then, suddenly, in the twinkling of an eye, Christ will split the sky, and God's great plan for the future will suddenly take center stage. It could be tomorrow. *It could be today!*

Esther: A Woman of Strength and Dignity

Christ made His appearance on an ordinary day, and His second appearance will be the same. What if it's today?

_____

_____

LORD, KEEP ME BALANCED

Give me neither poverty nor riches! Give me just enough to satisfy my needs.
PROVERBS 30:8

The longer I live, the more I realize the ease with which we can slip into extremes. I see it all around me and sometimes, to my own embarrassment, I find it in myself. A major prayer of mine as I grow older is, "Lord, keep me balanced!"

We need a balance between work and play, between kindness and firmness, between waiting and praying, between saving and spending, between wanting too much and expecting too little, between warm acceptance and keen discernment, between grace and truth.

For many folks, the struggle with imbalance is not an annual conflict—it's a daily grind. . . . The adversary of our souls is the expert of extremes. He never runs out of ways to push us to the limit . . . to get us to go so far out on one end we . . . cast perspective to the winds.

The longer I live, the more I must fight the tendency to go to extremes . . . and the more I value balance.

Living Beyond the Daily Grind

In what areas is your life most likely to get off-balance, and what safeguards do you put in place to prevent it?

_____

_____

NO ONE IS INSIGNIFICANT

The way of the righteous is like the first gleam of dawn,
which shines ever brighter until the full light of day.
PROVERBS 4:18

H ave you ever noticed how uniquely adapted each animal is to its environ-
ment and its way of life? On land, a duck waddles along ungainly on its
webbed feet. In the water, it glides along smooth as glass. The rabbit runs with
ease and great bursts of speed, but I've never seen one swimming laps.

God has placed you in His family and given you a certain mixture that
makes you unique. No mixture is insignificant!

That mix pleases Him completely. Nobody else is exactly like you. That
should bring you pleasure too.

When you operate in your realm of capabilities, you will excel and the whole
Body will benefit. . . . And you will experience incredible satisfaction.

The Finishing Touch

How has God specifically gifted you, and how do you use those gifts to
bring Him glory?

_____

_____

_____

_____

ACCOUNTABLE TO EACH OTHER

If you listen to correction, you grow in understanding.
PROVERBS 15:32

P eople who are accountable usually have four qualities:

Vulnerability—capable of being wounded, shown to be wrong, even admitting it before being confronted.

Teachability—a willingness to learn, being quick to hear and respond to reproof, being open to counsel.

Availability—accessible, touchable, able to be interrupted.

Honesty—committed to the truth regardless of how much it hurts, a willingness to admit the truth no matter how difficult or humiliating the admission may be. Hating all that is phony or false.

That's a tough list! . . . Today we need others to hold us accountable. Sometimes an objective opinion will reveal a blind spot. Sometimes we may simply need a sounding board to help keep us on target. Just remember—not one of us is an island. We need one another.

Living Above the Level of Mediocrity

Who in your life has permission to hold you accountable? Are you transparent with them about your struggles?

_____

_____

_____

277

PRAISING PERSONAL WORTH

*The words of the godly are a life-giving fountain. . . . Wise
words come from the lips of people with understanding.*
PROVERBS 10:11, 13

When we say thank-you to someone who completes a task, we are expressing our appreciation. But when we acknowledge and express our gratitude for what others are—in character, in motive, in heart—we are affirming them personally. A mark of maturity is the ability to affirm, not just appreciate.

How easy to see people (especially family members and fellow employees) as doers of tasks, but a task-oriented mentality is incomplete. As important as appreciation for a job well done may be, it too is incomplete. People aren't human tools appointed to accomplish a set of tasks, but human beings with souls, with feelings. How essential it is to recognize and affirm the unseen, hidden qualities that make an individual a person of worth and dignity.

Laugh Again

How can you take the time to affirm the worth and beauty of the people around you?

_____

_____

_____

Finding Fulfillment

The way of the godly leads to life; that path does not lead to death.
Proverbs 12:28

The ad campaigns that come through all the media channels promise much more than they can deliver. Their titillating messages fall into four categories: fortune and fame, power and pleasure.

Fortune. Fame. Power. Pleasure. The messages bombard us from every direction. But what's missing in all this? Stop and ask yourself that question. Isn't something very significant absent here?

You bet. A *vertical* dimension. There's not even a hint of God's will or what pleases Him in the hard-core pursuit of success. Note also that nothing in that horizontal list guarantees satisfaction or brings relief deep within the heart. And in the final analysis, what most people really want in life is contentment, fulfillment, and satisfaction.

Hope Again

Have you recently fallen into the trap of seeking fulfillment in earthly pleasures or possessions? If so, how can you pursue the better path?

_____

_____

_____

Focus First on God

I will thank the Lord because he is just; I will sing
praise to the name of the Lord Most High.
Psalm 7:17

There is a mystery, an aura about the living God that is designed to force us to trust Him, even when we cannot figure Him out (which is most of the time).

The mystery is purposeful, because His overall plan is profound. . . . His plan is not designed to make us comfortable; it's designed to make us more like Christ, to conform us to His will.

In this life, we have focus choices. We can focus on ourselves, we can focus on our circumstances, we can focus on other people, or we can focus on God. When you think biblically you focus first on God. Regardless of what you want, regardless of the circumstances you're under, regardless of what others say or think, regardless of how you feel, God and God alone is working out His great plan. And in the final tally, it will be fabulous!

The Mystery of God's Will

Where is your focus today? Are your eyes fixed on God and God alone?

_____

_____

_____

GET OUT OF THE RUT

A cheerful heart is good medicine, but a broken spirit saps a person's strength.
PROVERBS 17:22

Even though our workweek is decreasing and our weekend time is increasing, our country lacks inner peace. External leisure does not guarantee internal rest, does it? Time on our hands, we have. But we don't have meaningful "rest" in the biblical sense of the term.

The answer is to make a radical break with the rut of normal living. My good friend Tim Hansel suggests taking different kinds of vacations: mini-vacations (two minutes or more!). Change your routine, my friend. Blow the dust of boredom off your schedule. Shake yourself loose and get a taste of fresh life. Here are several suggestions for adding "zip" to your leisure:

- Begin jogging and/or an exercise program.
- Buy a bicycle and start pedaling.
- Enroll in a local art class.
- Take up a new hobby.
- Dig around in the soil or plant a small garden.

Strengthening Your Grip

When was the last time you did something out of the ordinary just for the pleasure of it? What mini-vacation can you take today?

_____

_____

GOD REIGNS OVER ALL

The LORD directs our steps, so why try to understand everything along the way?
PROVERBS 20:24

Stop and think for a moment about the word *sovereignty*. There's a small word nestled in the heart of it, the word *reign*: sove-*reign*-ty.

Sovereignty means our all-wise, all-knowing God reigns in realms beyond our comprehension to bring about a plan beyond our ability to alter, hinder, or stop.

Let me go further. His plan includes all promotions and demotions. His plan can mean both adversity and prosperity, tragedy and calamity, ecstasy and joy. . . . His plan is at work when we cannot imagine why, because it is so unpleasant, as much as when the reason is clear and pleasant. His sovereignty, though it is inscrutable, has dominion over all handicaps, all heartaches, all helpless moments. . . . Even when we cannot explain the reasons, He understands. And when we cannot see the end, He is there, nodding, "Yes, that is My plan."

The Mystery of God's Will

How exhausting is it to try to understand and explain all the ways of God? How can you rest in His perfect will instead?

_____

_____

_____

TRUST GOD FOR THE NEXT STEP

We can make our plans, but the LORD determines our steps.

PROVERBS 16:9

Let me pass along an old motto of mine. It's guided me for well more than thirty years and remains as appropriate now as the day it first slapped me alongside the head.

I try; I fail.

I trust; He succeeds!

Isn't that true? What simple counsel. Only eight words, yet how profound. Bottom line: If you are moving in the energy of the flesh, you're doomed to fail. The old hymn says it well: "The arm of flesh will fail you; you cannot trust your own." . . . But when you trust the Lord God to give you the next step, when you wait in humility upon Him, *He* will open the doors or close them, and you'll get to rest and relax until He says, "Go."

Moses: A Man of Selfless Dedication

Have you been trying to live on your own strength? How is it more beneficial for you to live in God's strength?

_____

_____

_____

_____

MORAL PURITY

People ruin their lives by their own foolishness and then are angry at the LORD.
PROVERBS 19:3

It is impossible to come to terms with moral purity without dealing with some practical facts related to the body—our flesh-and-blood appetites that crave satisfaction. Volumes are written about the mind, our emotional makeup, our "inner man," the soul, the spirit, and the spiritual dimension. But by comparison, very little is being said by evangelicals today about the physical body.

We are to present our bodies as living sacrifices to God (Romans 12:1).

We are instructed *not* to yield any part of our bodies as instruments of unrighteousness to sin (Romans 6:12–13).

Our bodies are actually "parts of Christ"; they belong to Him (1 Corinthians 6:15).

You see, these bodies of ours can easily lead us off course. It isn't that the body itself is evil; it's just that it possesses any number of appetites that are ready to respond to the surrounding stimuli . . . all of which are terribly appealing and temporarily satisfying.

Strengthening Your Grip

What physical temptations do you struggle with today? Have you asked the Lord for His strength to stand firm?

_____

_____

PERSPECTIVES AND PREFERENCES

So then, let us aim for harmony in the church and try to build each other up.
ROMANS 14:19

Disagreements are inevitable. . . . There will always be opposing viewpoints and a variety of perspectives on most subjects. Tastes differ as well as preferences. That is why they make vanilla and chocolate and strawberry ice cream, why they build Fords and Chevys, Chryslers and Cadillacs, Hondas and Toyotas. That is why our nation has room for Democrats and Republicans, conservatives and liberals—and moderates. The tension is built into our system. It is what freedom is all about, including religious freedom. I am fairly firm in my theological convictions, but that doesn't mean you (or anyone) must agree with me. All this explains why I place so much importance on leaving "wobble room" in our relationships. One's theological persuasion may not bend, but one's involvements with others must.

The Grace Awakening

Do you leave room in relationships for people to think differently than you? How can you contribute to harmony in the church?

_____

_____

_____

_____

GENUINE ENJOYMENT

For who can eat or enjoy anything apart from him?
ECCLESIASTES 2:25

When I was growing up, my family lived next door to a family that had many of the world's goods we didn't have, but they didn't have the joys Christ can bring—which we had in abundance. I remember one Christmas when we were singing together as a family.

Suddenly, my mom said, "We're making so much noise; we better close the windows or we'll disturb all the neighbors." So we closed the windows.

Within minutes our phone rang. It was a girl who lived next door. She asked, "Why'd you close the windows?"

"Well, we didn't want to disturb you," was my mom's answer. The girl blurted out, "Disturb us? That's the most laughter we've heard the entire Christmas season! . . . That's beautiful music!"

If you really want to have fun—I mean the kind of fun that is really enjoyment (without a hangover)—then you need . . . a relationship with the living God.

Living on the Ragged Edge

How has your relationship with Christ brought a joy to your life that endures through any hardship and trial?

_____

_____

WE'RE ALL CLAY POTS

But we ourselves are like fragile clay jars containing this great treasure.

2 CORINTHIANS 4:7

Do you know what an earthen vessel is? It's nothing more than a clay pot.... That's a reference to our bodies and our abilities in the strength of our flesh. That is all you and I have to offer God . . . a pot. A perishable container.

You may be like brittle, delicate china. You break and chip easily, and you could show the glue marks because of those broken times. Then again, you may be a rugged, scarred hunk of heavy pottery—not very attractive, but boy, are you useful. Or you may be composed of clay that hasn't yet been fired in the kiln; you are still being molded and shaped for use.

To tell you the truth, it isn't the condition of the pot that's most important. What's important is the treasure inside—the light and glory of Christ's salvation. What's a few dings, or even a crack or two? If others can see the glory inside through the cracks, so much the better.

Moses: A Man of Selfless Dedication

Are you living as if you truly believe that you carry a great treasure within you?

_____

_____

_____

287

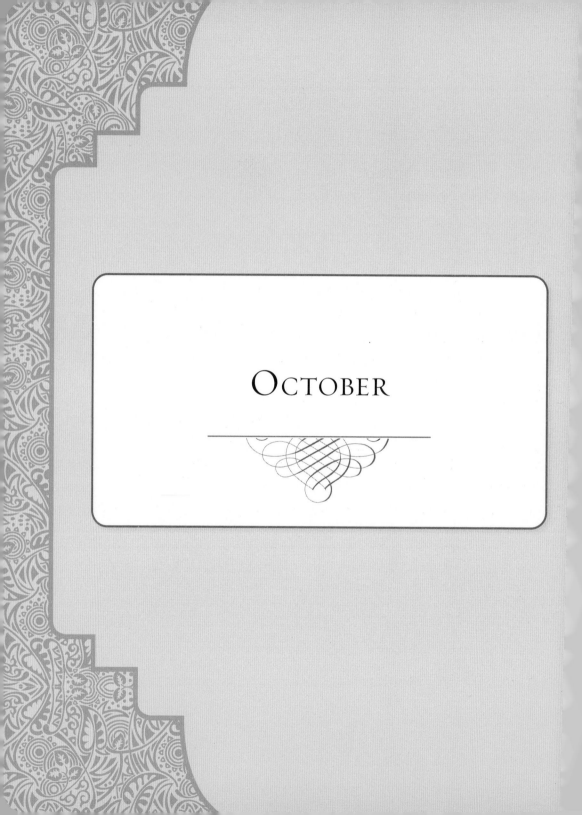

OCTOBER

SINCERE FAITH AT HOME

I remember your genuine faith, for you share the faith that first filled your grandmother Lois and your mother, Eunice.

2 TIMOTHY 1:5

Paul knew Timothy's heritage. He knew that the things that characterized the grandmother and the mother characterized Timothy. That's the way sincere faith works.

Listen to this, moms! Please read my words carefully. A church, a Christian school, a circle of Christian friends can deposit facts into heads. But they cannot translate truth into authentic living. Those avenues can't make it "real." Truth doesn't weave itself into real fleshed-out life until it flows through you. Kids gather the facts. They learn them from the books. They see it in print on a page. But then they look to you to see it modeled into a sincere kind of faith.

Believe me, we can give our children the words to say, we can convey Christian concepts until we turn a deep shade of blue, but they won't fit reality until our young see the reality of such truths in the home.

Growing Wise in Family Life

In what ways was godly living modeled for you as you grew up? Are you modeling it for your children now?

_____

_____

_____

IN THE SHADOW OF THE SAVIOR

Trust in the LORD and do good.
PSALM 37:3

I f you wish to be a man or woman of God who desires to live a godly life that will leave its mark upon this world, you must stand in the shadow of your Savior. Trust Him to work through the trials you encounter, through the extreme circumstances you cannot handle on your own. He is still the God of impossible situations. He does what no earthly individual can do.

You must approach the impossible with calmness and contentment, with gentleness and self-control, with faith and humility.

Examine your own life for these character traits and take them one by one before God. You might say . . . "Lord, today I want to do what You say regarding contentment; I want to have a calm and gentle spirit. I don't simply want to call myself a Christian. . . . Help me this day to face everything and deal with everyone with a gentle and quiet spirit. Help me to be content, even though I don't get things my way."

That is how we personify a life of faith.

Elijah: A Man of Heroism & Humility

As you look at where the Lord has you today, how can you trust Him more and how can you do good?

_____

_____

GOD DOES MYSTERIOUS THINGS

I realized that no one can discover everything God is doing under the sun.

ECCLESIASTES 8:17

There are numerous riddles in life that remain wrapped in mystery and shrouded inside an enigma. The sea, for example, is an unexplainable phenomenon. . . . There are diseases that still remain a mystery . . . yet we seem to have little trouble going on through life with dozens of riddles still unanswered, hundreds of mysteries still unsolved.

But when God leaves us with a mystery that isn't solved in a week or two, most of us go through desperate struggles believing that He is good or fair. I mean, after all, if we're going to trust a good God, He should do only good things, right? No fair doing mysterious stuff!

Yet God's Word, like God's will, is full of mysteries. Why should we be surprised, then, when God steps in and does mysterious things? Why should that make us wonder if He is good—or wonder if we want to keep believing? Since when must everything be easily or logically explained?

Living on the Ragged Edge

Do you struggle with the mysterious ways of God? What if, instead, you trusted His goodness?

_____

_____

_____

DON'T EXPECT APPROVAL

*"Look! I am about to cover the earth with a flood. . . . But I
will confirm my covenant with you. So enter the boat."*
GENESIS 6:17–18

God informed Noah of His plan: He was going to destroy the world with
a flood. So for one hundred and twenty years, by faith, Noah followed
the Lord's leading. He gathered the materials, he built the ark, probably to the
ridicule of everyone around him. After all, this was a world that had never
known rain; the earth was watered from beneath. And while Noah was building
this ark, he was preaching righteousness to those around him. . . . Surrounded
and mocked by his depraved . . . contemporaries, this preacher of righteousness,
by faith, stood against the tide of his culture.

Sometimes our faith is such a rebuke to our peers that we suffer persecution
because of it. No extra charge for his simple warning: Don't expect overwhelming approval and affirmation just because you've chosen to walk by faith.

The Mystery of God's Will

Have you suffered ridicule or rebuke for your faith? How does it help to
know that Christ Himself endured the same?

_____

_____

_____

IN THE WORLD, NOT OF IT

Do not love this world nor the things it offers you.
1 JOHN 2:15

I f you want to stay clean, even when you're walking alone in the dark, low-ceilinged coal mine of the corrupt and secular culture, you need to remember a few practical things—four come to mind.

1. *Pay close attention to what you look at. . . .* Our eyes seem to be the closest connection to our minds.
2. *Give greater thought to the consequences of sin than to its pleasures. . . .* Nobody ever mentions the ugly underside of pleasurable sins.
3. *Begin each day by renewing your sense of reverence for God.* Start each new day by talking to the Lord, even if that early morning talk has to be brief.
4. *Periodically during each day focus fully on Christ. . . .* Imagine Him as He is thinking about you, praying for you, standing with you, living in you.

Be *in* the world but not *of* it.

Hope Again

What daily practices do you have in place to keep your heart devoted to the Lord and not distracted by the world?

_____

_____

GOD IS TRUSTWORTHY

"My thoughts are nothing like your thoughts," says the LORD.
"And my ways are far beyond anything you could imagine."
ISAIAH 55:8

God is the Potter; we are the clay. He's the Shepherd; we are the sheep. He's the Master; we are the servant. No matter how educated we are, no matter how much power and influence we may think we have, no matter how long we have walked with Him, no matter how significant we may imagine ourselves to be in His plan . . . none of that qualifies us to grasp the first particle of why He does what He does when He does it and how He chooses to do it.

The amazing thing is that even in the midst of disappointment, surprise, and mystery you will discover how very reliable and trustworthy God is—and how secure you are in His hands.

Puzzling as the process may be to us, He stays with His plan. There is no need for us to know all the reasons, and He certainly doesn't need to explain Himself. Potters work with the clay; they don't fret over it . . . or ask permission to remake the clay into whatever they wish.

The Mystery of God's Will

When you think about mistakes you've made, aren't you glad that God's ways are so much higher than yours?

_____

_____

CHOOSE JOY!

"You will live in joy and peace."
ISAIAH 55:12

How do we live with worry and stress and fear? How do we withstand these joy stealers?

Let me be downright practical and tell you what I do. First I remind myself early in the morning and on several occasions during the day, "God, You are at work, and You are in control. And, Lord God, You know this is happening. You were there at the beginning, and You will bring everything that occurs to a conclusion that results in Your greater glory in the end." And then? Then (and *only* then!) I relax. From that point on, it really doesn't matter all that much what happens. It's in God's hands.

The pressure on you may be intense. A half dozen joy stealers may be waiting outside your door, ready to pounce at the first opportunity. However, nothing can rob you of your hold on grace, your claim to peace, or your confidence in God without your permission. Choose joy. Never release your grip!

Laugh Again

Do you make it a regular habit to preach the truth of the gospel to yourself? If not, why not begin today?

_____

_____

_____

MERCY FOR THE MISERABLE

*"God blesses those who are persecuted for doing right,
for the Kingdom of Heaven is theirs."*
MATTHEW 5:10

Mercy is a concern for people in need. It has to do with assisting those less fortunate than ourselves, including those who suffer the consequences of disappointment, disease, and distress. One of my mentors used to say, "Mercy is God's ministry to the miserable." And it does not stop with compassion or sadness over someone in dire straits; it means identifying with those who are hurting and imagining the pain they are having to endure, and then doing something about it.

It's not simply some feeling of sympathy or sadness over somebody in trouble, but really getting inside the other person's skin, feeling what *they* feel, understanding *their* misery, and then helping them through it.

Simple Faith

How can you extend mercy to those hurting around you? How can you lean in and feel their pain?

_____

_____

_____

_____

LET GOD OPEN THE DOORS

Those who fear the LORD are secure; he will be a refuge for their children.
PROVERBS 14:26

Do you find yourself trying to hammer a square peg into a round hole? Are you pushing and straining and dumping loads of emotional freight to get something going? You'd better call time-out and check with the Coach! When God's in something, it flows.

Let's say you have it in your heart to get into some kind of ministry at your place of employment. You'd like the opportunity to sit down with some co-workers and maybe spend fifteen minutes together around the Scriptures at lunch. Great idea! But don't force it. Lay it before God and let Him open the doors. If He is in it, it's remarkable how approval will be granted, how a growing interest will percolate, and how the timing will fall right into place. It will come together almost in spite of you.

God has no limitations in His ability to pull something off, but He's going to do it in His time and not before.

Moses: A Man of Selfless Dedication

Do you have a ministry you want to pursue? Have you spent time praying and seeking God's will in the matter?

_____

_____

_____

FLEXIBLE AND WILLING

Imitate God, therefore, in everything you do, because you are his dear children.
EPHESIANS 5:1–2

God says we are to be "imitators" of Him, which really means we are to "mimic" Him. Since God is a God of freshness and change, so we should be.

Are you open to change in your life? Are you willing to risk? Are you flexible enough to innovate? Are you willing to tolerate the sheer possibility of making a massive change in your direction for life? "Lord, is it South America? Great! Or Indonesia? I'll do it. I'll move or change my profession. Fine! Are You leading me into a new venture? I'll do it. Count me in!"

That's the spirit! It may mean moving across the street. It may mean moving across the States. It may mean moving across the seas. How flexible are you? It may not involve a move at all, only a willingness.

Living Above the Level of Mediocrity

What changes, big or small, is the Lord leading you to make in your life?

_____

_____

_____

_____

_____

GOD LOVES US STILL

"I have loved you, my people, with an everlasting love.
With unfailing love I have drawn you to myself."

JEREMIAH 31:3

F rom a distance, we dazzle; up close, we're tarnished. Put enough of us together and we may resemble an impressive mountain range. But when you get down into the shadowy crevices . . . the Alps we ain't.

That's why our Lord means so much to us. He is intimately acquainted with all our ways. Darkness and light are alike to Him. No one of us is hidden from His sight. All things are open and laid bare before Him: our darkest secret, our deepest shame, our stormy past, our worst thought, our hidden motive, our vilest imagination . . . even our vain attempts to cover the ugly with snow-white beauty.

He sees it all. He knows our frame. He remembers we are dust.

Best of all, He loves us still.

The Finishing Touch

What is that one thing that you think makes you unlovable? The Lord knows all about it and loves you anyway.

_____

_____

_____

BIBLICAL THINKING

Wickedness never brings stability, but the godly have deep roots.
PROVERBS 12:3

I want to be quite direct with you. Secular thought has taken a tragic toll on the servant of God's distinctiveness. This has begun to influence the church. Many a believer has surrendered his mind to the world's system. The uniquely Christian mind, therefore, is a rare find. Humanism, secularism, intellectualism, and materialism have invaded our thinking to such a marked degree our testimony has become diluted—in some cases, nonexistent.

Influenced and impressed by the press, our secularized system of education, shallow social expectations, and the quasi-omnipotent forces of conformity to peer pressure (not to mention the impact of television and movies), Christian servants can easily be caught in the trap. We can literally stop thinking biblically.

Take heed!

Improving Your Serve

How can you ensure you're letting the Word, and not the world, influence and shape your thinking on social and church issues?

_____

_____

_____

_____

GOD'S PASTURES ARE GREEN

We are his people, the sheep of his pasture.

PSALM 100:3

I am told that sheep, being stupid animals, frequently are alarmed and actually run over each other, racing away from something that startles them. The shepherd corrects the problem by catching a sheep and gently, yet firmly, forcing it to lie down and feed quietly on the grass beneath its feet.

In our hectic, hurried, harassed age in which headache medications have become the best-selling national product, we must occasionally be made to lie down by our Shepherd-Savior. When He steps into our helter-skelter world, He often forces us to rest. If that has occurred in your life, give thanks—the pastures are green!

Living Beyond the Daily Grind

When have you benefited from the Lord forcing you to rest?

_____

_____

_____

_____

_____

_____

STOP RUNNING SCARED

But you, O Lord, are a shield around me; you are my
glory, the one who holds my head high.
PSALM 3:3

Did you know that you operate at your poorest when you are scared? A little fear is good for us when danger is present, but a lot of it is demoralizing. It takes away the hope, the dream, the vision, the possibility of overcoming.

Fears lurk in the shadows of every area of life. Perhaps you've suddenly discovered that an unexpected addition to your family is on the way. . . . You may be uncertain where your job is leading. . . . You are uneasy about what's around the corner. Or perhaps you have a doctor's appointment pending, and you are afraid of what the exam might reveal. Jesus says, "Stop being afraid. Trust Me!"

Jesus Christ stands at the door. He holds out His hands that are scarred. His feet are pierced, and He bears in His body the marks of death. He says, "I know the pressure you are under. I understand the strain. I know the unfair abuse. But let Me offer you some encouragement. Don't be afraid. Look at life through My eyes! Stop letting life intimidate you! Stop running scared. Trust Me!"

Perfect Trust

Are you letting fear hold you back? What would you do and where would you go if you were unafraid?

_____

_____

THE SIGNIFICANCE OF ONE

"I looked for someone who might rebuild the wall . . .
someone to stand in the gap in the wall."
EZEKIEL 22:30

I n an overpopulated world, it's easy to underestimate the significance of one. There are so many people who have so many gifts and skills who are already doing so many things that are so important. Who needs me? What can I as one individual contribute to the overwhelming needs of our world? Sure is easy to let the vastness of our surroundings do a number on us, isn't it?

But the truth is, you are you—the only you in all the world. . . . You're the only person with your exact heritage, your precise series of events in the pilgrimage and sufferings of life that have brought you to this hour.

When I read God's Word I don't find that many stories about great crusades and . . . mass meetings where God's attention rested on an entire country or a whole community. More often, I find individual men and women who made a difference, who set the pace or cut a wide swath or stood in the gap and changed their times.

Esther: A Woman of Strength and Dignity

God created you to be, not just one of many, but a uniquely gifted individual. What task has He called you to accomplish in His name?

_____

_____

STILL AND QUIET STREAMS

The LORD is my shepherd. . . . He leads me beside peaceful streams.
PSALM 23:1–2

H e leads me beside peaceful streams." Look at that phrase. Literally, it refers to waters that have been stilled. Mentally capture the peaceful scene. The sheep are weary and worn. They need a long, refreshing drink from the rapid stream nearby. But sheep are instinctively afraid of running water. . . . Though tired and hot from a blistering day, thirsty sheep will only stand and stare at the fast-flowing stream but never drink.

The shepherd then steps in. With his rod and staff he loosens a few large stones and dams up a place, causing the rushing waters to slow their current. The now quiet waters immediately attract the sheep. In the midst of a rushing stream the shepherd has provided refreshment for the flock with water he has stilled.

Has your Shepherd done this? Has He recently stepped in and made those busy currents of your life a source of refreshment by stilling them, by bringing order out of chaos?

Living Beyond the Daily Grind

How has God stilled the rushing waters of your life in order to give you peace and rest in a busy world?

_____

_____

ABUNDANT LIFE

"My purpose is to give them a rich and satisfying life."
JOHN 10:10

Because it is short, life is packed with challenging possibilities. Because it is uncertain, it's filled with challenging adjustments. I'm convinced that's much of what Jesus meant when He promised us an abundant life. Abundant with challenges, running over with possibilities, filled with opportunities to adapt, shift, alter, and change. Come to think of it, that's the secret of staying young. It's also the path that leads to optimism and motivation.

With each new dawn, life delivers a package to your front door, rings your doorbell, and runs. Each package is cleverly wrapped in paper and big print. One package reads: "Watch out. Better worry about this!" Another: "Danger. This will bring fear!" And another: "Impossible. You'll never handle this one!"

When you hear that ring tomorrow morning, try something new. Have Jesus Christ answer the door.

The Finishing Touch

Are you experiencing an abundant life or enduring an abundant load? Do you need to hand your burden over to the Lord?

_____

_____

_____

EYES TRAINED ON GOD

He is faithful and just to forgive us our sins.
1 JOHN 1:9

Perhaps the words "very low" paint a picture of bleakness that describes you at this very moment. You have ignored God's warnings and pushed your strong convictions aside as you associated with the wrong crowd. But now you are at the end of your rope. You're discouraged. You have failed miserably. You're thinking, *What a terrible way to live!*

All of us have spent time in that miserable camp called Reaping What Was Sown. En route, there's enough pleasure to make it seem like fun, but when it's all said and done, it's downright awful.

What we need are suggestions that get us back on track. First, you need to openly acknowledge what caused your condition. Openly admit that you have failed to stand alone as a true child of God.

Second, you will not stand alone when outnumbered or stand tall when tested or stand firm when discouraged if your focus remains on the odds. Your eyes must be trained on the Lord. Everything depends on your focus.

Living Above the Level of Mediocrity

Are you burdened with shame over sinful choices? Why not confess them and accept the forgiveness that is yours in Christ?

_____

_____

SUFFERING SIMPLIFIES LIFE

*But as for me, how good it is to be near God! I have
made the Sovereign LORD my shelter.*

PSALM 73:28

Trials put our faith to the test.

No matter what its source or intensity, there's something about suffering that simplifies life and draws us back to the basics. Invariably, especially during a time of intense trial . . . I go back to what I really believe. I return to the elementals such as prayer and dependence, like getting quiet and waiting on God. I remind myself, *God is sovereign. . . . This is no accident. He has a plan and a purpose.* Those thoughts give us hope beyond our trials.

Trials put our faith to the test as well as stretch our confidence in Him. They force us back to the bedrock of faith upon which our foundation rests, and this becomes a refining and necessary process.

Hope Again

What fundamentals of your faith do you need to return to during difficult seasons? What brings you comfort in times of trouble?

_____

_____

_____

_____

SIMPLY AND SILENTLY

The LORD is good to those who depend on him, to those who search for him.
LAMENTATIONS 3:25

S pend a full day in quietness. Sundays are great days to do that. Set aside at least part of the afternoon to be completely quiet. Meditation is sometimes a lost art in this modern, hurry-up world. I suggest you revive it. Not by endlessly repeating some mantra to get into some other frame of mind. Not that. Simply and silently wait before your faithful God. Read a passage of Scripture, perhaps a psalm, and let it speak. Say nothing. Just sit silently. Let Him talk. Let Him reassure you that you are fully and completely forgiven and that your shame is gone. Feel His arms reach around you. . . . Feel again the freshness and relief of His presence.

The Mystery of God's Will

When was the last time (if ever!) you sat completely silent for an extended period of time before the Lord?

_____

_____

_____

_____

_____

THE PLAN IN A CHILD'S HEART

*Though good advice lies deep within the heart, a
person with understanding will draw it out.*

PROVERBS 20:5

To make this verse even more practical, let's think of this "plan" in these terms: "A plan in the heart of a child is like deep water, but a parent of understanding draws it out."

Do you have a child who is mechanically inclined? He needs to know you notice. Make comments about it. Brag on his ability. Do you have a child who is athletic, well-coordinated? He needs to know you believe he is well-coordinated. You say, "That's obvious." But perhaps he hasn't heard it directly from you. He wants to hear you *say it*. You have a child who is intellectually gifted? You sense that she would be good at research, probing deeply into various subjects? *Tell her*. Mention the future possibilities. Help her find the right university. Rather than hammering away on petty stuff that doesn't matter, spend more time discovering how your children's interests can be channeled. Building a strong self-esteem takes a commitment to discover.

Growing Wise in Family Life

Do you hold back affirmation because you think your child already knows his giftedness? Why not say the words today?

_____

_____

MARK YOUR MEETING PLACE

I long for the Lord more than sentries long for the dawn.
PSALM 130:6

To meet regularly with God, you need a place. The house in which I was reared was very small. My mom's place to meet with God was the bathroom. She put her books near the little stove that heated the room. When she met with God she put a little sign on the door that said, "Do not disturb."

Busy mothers can't have their time with the Lord at breakfast or suppertime. That creates havoc. . . . So if you're a mother, you have to be practical about this. Choose a time that works for you, but remember, you need time with God.

If you're a businessperson, your best place might be at your office. I know a businessman who goes to his office early every weekday morning just so he can spend time with the Lord. . . .

Where is your place? You need such a place where you can sit down and enjoy some uninterrupted fellowship with your Lord. I warn you, if you don't arrange an appropriate place, you probably won't meet regularly with God.

Moses: A Man of Selfless Dedication

Where do you meet with the Lord? If you don't have a designated place, why not create one today?

_____

_____

FREE OF ANXIETY

Now hear my prayer; listen to my cry.
PSALM 88:2

Our minds can be kept free of anxiety as we dump the load of our cares on the Lord in prayer. By getting rid of the stuff that drags us down, we create space for joy to take its place.

Think of it like this: Circumstances occur that could easily crush us. They may originate on the job or at home or even during the weekend when we are relaxing. Unexpectedly, they come. Immediately we have a choice to make . . . an attitude choice. We can hand the circumstances to God and ask Him to take control, or we can roll up our mental sleeves and slug it out. Joy awaits our decision.

Strengthening Your Grip

Is your tendency to bear a burden as long as you can? How can you begin turning it over to the Lord immediately?

_____

_____

_____

_____

_____

TAKE HEART!

*For God is not unjust. He will not forget how hard you have
worked for him and how you have shown your love to him.*
HEBREWS 6:10

I t is so easy to feel used and unappreciated.
Do I write to you who serve behind the scenes in a ministry or a business?
You work faithfully and diligently, yet the glory goes to another. Your efforts
make someone else successful. How easy to feel resentful! Assistant directors,
associate and assistant pastors, administrative assistants, "internal personnel."
All members of the I-work-hard-but-because-I'm-not-up-front-I-never-get-the-
credit club, *take heart!* Our God who rewards in secret will never overlook your
commitment.

Keep a close eye on your pride. God's true servant is like the Lord Jesus,
who "came not to be served but to serve others and to give his life as a ransom
for many" (Mark 10:45). . . . When you make the stew and someone else gets the
strokes, remember your role: to serve and to give.

Improving Your Serve

How can you guard your spirit from becoming bitter as you live a life of
service?

_____

_____

_____

Do Little Things Well

For their command is a lamp and their instruction a light;
their corrective discipline is the way to life.

PROVERBS 6:23

If you want to be a person with a large vision, you must cultivate the habit of doing the little things well. That's when God puts iron in your bones! . . . The test of my calling is not how well I do before the public on Sunday; it's how carefully I cover the bases Monday through Saturday when there's nobody to check up on me, when nobody is looking.

When God develops character, He works on it throughout a lifetime. He's never in a hurry.

It is in the schoolroom of solitude and obscurity that we learn to become men and women of God. It is from the schoolmasters of monotony and reality that we learn to "king it." That's how we become—like David—men and women after God's own heart.

David: A Man of Passion and Destiny

How has God been working on you behind the scenes—in places no one else sees?

_____

_____

_____

THE RESPONSE OF WORSHIP

God might kill me, but I have no other hope.
JOB 13:15

The more impossible the situation, the greater God accomplishes His work. This truth is no better illustrated than in the life of Job, a man who went through great times of suffering until God finally brought rest and restoration. When I read the account of Job's plight, I cannot imagine it. He lost every-thing he owned—his home, all ten of his children, and the loss of his health. It is probably safe to say that not one of us has ever entered into such depths of misery and calamity. Remarkably, his first response to God was the response of worship. "Job got up, tore his robe, and shaved his head; then he fell to the ground and worshiped" (Job 1:20 NASB).

You might expect him to fall to the ground and cry for mercy or to rant and rave that these back-to-back events were simply not fair. But he didn't. He worshipped. And not because he understood what was happening to him, but in spite of all that was happening to him. Not only did Job worship, he accepted what God had sent into his life. That is wisdom.

Perfect Trust

Do you withhold worship until you understand what is happening? Or, like Job, do you worship knowing that God is in control?

_____

_____

DISCERNMENT AND COURAGE

*Search for [commands] as you would for silver; seek them like hidden
treasures. Then you will understand what it means to fear the LORD.*
PROVERBS 2:4–5

To have the discernment it takes to refuse the sinful, faith must overshadow
feelings.

My feelings say, "Try it!" Faith says, "Stay away from it."

My feelings say, "Give it up. Throw in the towel." Faith says, "Hold on!"

We live in a day of feelings. "Whatever you *feel* like, get at it." The Academy
Award-winning song a few decades back captured that philosophy with the
words, "It can't be wrong, when it feels so right. . . ." Oh, yes, it can! Faith says,
"Hold it. You have come to a fork in the road. If you take that journey, you will
buy into a lifestyle that is wrong. Stop. Back up. Look again."

Maybe you find yourself right there. You have already made some poor
choices. If so, it's time to back up. . . . Retrace your steps right back to that place
where you made the wrong turn. That takes discernment and courage.

Moses: A Man of Selfless Dedication

How do you live out your faith in a world that tells you to follow your
feelings? What practical steps can you take to stay on the right path?

_____

_____

_____

GENUINE ENCOURAGEMENT

*Everyone enjoys a fitting reply; it is wonderful to
say the right thing at the right time!*

PROVERBS 15:23

All of us need encouragement—somebody to believe in us. To reassure and reinforce us. To help us pick up the pieces and go on. To provide us with increased determination in spite of the odds.

When we encourage others we spur them on, we stimulate and affirm them. It is helpful to remember the distinction between appreciation and affirmation. We appreciate what a person *does,* but we affirm who a person *is.* Appreciation comes and goes because it is usually related to something someone accomplishes. Affirmation goes deeper. It is directed to the person him- or herself.

I do not care how influential or secure or mature a person may appear to be; genuine encouragement never fails to help. Most of us need massive doses of it.

Strengthening Your Grip

Have you ever considered the difference between appreciation and affirmation? Are you offering both to those around you?

_____

_____

_____

_____

ACCOUNTABILITY IS WISE

[There is] a time to embrace and a time to turn away.
ECCLESIASTES 3:5

There are occasions when we need the embrace of a friend who pulls our head close and whispers in our ear words of understanding, encouraging us not to quit, reminding us that life will go on. . . . We will make it. Such embraces put steel into our bones. They help us make it through the night.

And then there are times when that same person may take us by the shoulders, hold us at arm's length, and confront us with the hard truth: "Now listen to this, I can't agree with you. I must be honest with you. . . . I think what you are doing is wrong." That is not a time for embracing. But for a life to stay balanced, both affirmation and accountability are needed.

The longer I live, the more I want to listen to wise people. Not so much intelligent people as wise people. A person who is wise not only has intelligence but understands life and can help put it all together.

Living on the Ragged Edge

Are you a person of wisdom who knows when to embrace and comfort and when to stand back and speak truth?

_____

_____

_____

A LISTENING HEART

"O my people, listen as I speak."
PSALM 50:7

M ark it down, things do not "just happen." Ours is not a random, whistle-in-the-dark universe. There is a God-arranged plan for this world of ours, which includes a specific plan for you. And through every ordinary day and every extraordinary moment, there is a God who constantly seeks you.

You're walking through [life] and you suddenly encounter one event among the countless events that happen every day and every night. All of a sudden, life changes. Something's different. And never doubt it! The God who loves us and redeemed us uses those moments to advance His purposes.

He doesn't speak vocally from heaven, shouting down His Word at you. He uses His Book, He uses His people, and He uses events in your life. And through the blending of those unusual events, He says, "Listen to Me. . . . Pay attention, and I will speak to you. Answer My call, and I will use you."

All that is needed are a hushed spirit and a listening heart.

Moses: A Man of Selfless Dedication

Do you feel that God has been silent in your recent time of trouble? Could it be that you simply aren't listening?

_____

_____

HELD IN HIGHEST REGARD

*The LORD your God will soon bring you into the land. . . . Be careful
not to forget the LORD, who rescued you from slavery.*
DEUTERONOMY 6:10, 12

G od's got our good at heart. After giving, giving, giving so many things,
He warns us about forgetting Him. How easy, when blessed, to adopt a
presumptuous, arrogant spirit. Indulgence begins an erosion within that leads
to indifference, which ultimately results in independence. "Who needs God any
longer?" It is an attitude often found among the self-sufficient. The secret of
keeping that from happening? "You shall fear only the LORD your God; and you
shall worship Him" (Deuteronomy 6:13 NASB).

When we maintain a sincere fear of God, something wonderful occurs
within. Self-made pride and presumption continue to decrease as fear of God
increases. I do not mean fright . . . feeling uneasy and afraid in His presence.
The right kind of fear is reverence for His holy name, a wholesome respect for
His sovereign will, holding Him in highest regard.

Growing Wise in Family Life

How can you make a regular habit of remembering all that the Lord has
done for you in the past?

_____

_____

GOD IS THERE AND HE IS NOT SILENT

Even though the actions of godly and wise people are in God's hands, no one knows whether God will show them favor.

ECCLESIASTES 9:1

Regardless of rank, status, color, creed, age, heritage, intelligence, or temperament, the "hand of God" is upon us. The late philosopher-theologian Francis Schaeffer was absolutely correct: "God is there and He is not silent." What reassurance this brings! It tells us, among other things, that nothing is out of control. Nor are we useless, despairing robots stumbling awkwardly through time and space, facing a bleak fate at the end. But neither does this mean we are given periodic briefings about His strategy.

Being in the hand of God is not synonymous with or a guarantee for being economically prosperous, physically healthy, protected from pain . . . and having everyone smile and appreciate us. What helps is the knowledge that behind whatever happens is a God who cares, who hasn't lost a handle on the controls.

Living on the Ragged Edge

Do you obey and serve the Lord out of love or with an expectation of immediate reward?

_____

_____

_____

NOVEMBER

GOD'S GRACIOUS LOVE

Let all that I am praise the LORD. . . . [He] crowns
me with love and tender mercies.
PSALM 103:1, 4

The sovereign Most High God is ruler over our lives. So it's obvious that if we ever have the feeling of relief, God has given it to us. He's the author of relief. He's the one who grants us the peace, the satisfaction, the ease. In fact, I think relief is a wonderful synonym for mercy. Mercy is God's active compassion, which He demonstrates to the miserable. When we are in a time of deep distress and God activates His compassion to bring about relief, we've experienced mercy.

The connecting link between a holy God and a sinful person is God's love, which activates His grace, which, in turn, sets in motion His mercy. They're like divine dominoes that bump up against one another. He loves us not because of something in ourselves but because of something in Himself. . . . Grace prompts mercy . . . and there it is: *relief!*

The Mystery of God's Will

When have you experienced the mercy of God in your life? Or the sudden relief during a painful season?

_____

_____

_____

"SOMEDAY" MAY NEVER COME

For everything there is a season, a time for every activity under heaven.
ECCLESIASTES 3:1

Remember me? I'm the guy who promotes waiting. Allowing the Lord to open the doors, clear the way, smooth the path, shove you through. You know, all the stuff you expect a preacher to say.

But I do think we can get so good at waiting that we never act. We yawn and passively mutter, "Maybe, someday" as we let opportunities slip away. Like having friends over for ice cream or going on a picnic. Like using the fine china or celebrating a birthday . . . or slipping away for a weekend of relaxation and romance . . . or sailing for a day . . . or spending a week away from the family. "Not this year . . . but maybe, someday . . ."

Don't wait! If you continue such passivity, someday will never come—and you'll regret it for the rest of your days.

Day by Day with Charles Swindoll

What have you been waiting to do? Perhaps today should be the day!

_____

_____

_____

_____

_____

THE PREPARATION PROCESS

For his unfailing love toward those who fear him is as great
as the height of the heavens above the earth.

PSALM 103:11

How does the servant of God cope when the bottom drops out? I have
found great help from two truths:

Nothing touches me that has not passed through the hands of my heavenly
Father. Nothing. Whatever occurs, God has sovereignly surveyed and approved.
We may not know why (we may *never* know why), but we do know our pain is
no accident to Him who guides our lives.

Everything I endure is designed to prepare me for serving others more
effectively. Everything. Since my heavenly Father is committed to shaping me
into the image of His Son, He knows the ultimate value of this painful experience. It is a necessary part of the preparation process. It is being used to empty
our hands of our own resources, our own sufficiency, and turn us back to Him—
the faithful Provider.

Improving Your Serve

Do you believe that God is aware of your every hurt? How does it help to
know that your pain has purpose?

_____

_____

_____

An Excellent Wife

Who can find a virtuous and capable wife? . . . Her husband praises her.
PROVERBS 31:10, 28

A wife is not responsible for her husband's life. She is responsible for her life. You cannot make your husband something he is not. Only God can do that.

I think it was the evangelist's wife, Ruth Graham, who once said, "It is my job to love Billy. It is God's job to make him good." I'd call that a wonderful philosophy for any wife to embrace.

Wife, it's your job to love your husband. It's God's job to change his life.

And wives who are truly obedient to Christ will find that He will honor their secure spirit.

Hope Again

Have you found yourself trying to be the Holy Spirit in someone else's life? What if you just loved them instead?

_____

_____

_____

_____

_____

_____

GOD'S IN CHARGE

"I create the light and make the darkness. I send good times and bad times. I, the LORD, am the one who does these things."

ISAIAH 45:7

I don't know why a tornado destroys one neighborhood and not another. I just know that even in this calamity God's plan is not frustrated or altered. Either that, or He isn't God. He isn't sitting on the edge of heaven, wondering what will happen next. That's not the God of the Scriptures. So while we cannot fathom the "Why?" of this age-old question, we do know that Scripture states that God is not surprised by calamity. Somehow or other, it's all part of His mysterious will.

Now that's a tough concept to justify. So my advice is quite simple: Quit trying. . . . Remember, nothing is a surprise to God, not even our slightest trials. His plan may seem unfair, humanly illogical, and lacking compassion, but that's because we dwell in the here and now. We lack the vertical view. . . . God's in charge, not us!

The Mystery of God's Will

In what situation do you need to quit trying to figure out the "why"? What if you just accepted that it is and trust God?

_____

_____

_____

An Unselfish Attitude

Don't be selfish; don't try to impress others. Be humble,
thinking of others as better than yourselves.
PHILIPPIANS 2:3

How is it possible to pull off an unselfish attitude when we find ourselves surrounded by quite the opposite? . . . Three practical ideas may help:
1. Never let selfishness or conceit be your motive. That's right, *never.*
2. Always regard others as more important than yourself. Though this is not a natural trait, it can become a habit—and what an important one!
3. Don't limit your attention to your own personal interest—include others.

Some may try to dissuade you from what may appear to be an unbalanced, extremist position. They may tell you that anyone who adopts this sort of attitude is getting dangerously near self-flagellation and a loss of healthy self-esteem. Nonsense! The goal is that we become so interested in others and in helping them reach their highest good that we become self-forgetful in the process.

Laugh Again

Are the majority of your concerns over the course of a day about yourself or others?

_____

_____

ENOUGH IS ENOUGH

True humility and fear of the LORD lead to riches, honor, and long life.
PROVERBS 22:4

I'm not interested in how much you make or what choices you make regarding your lifestyle. Who am I to judge another? My concern really has nothing to do with what you own but rather with why you own it. . . . Can you honestly say that your heart is not fixed on tangible treasures? Is your giving generous? Do you readily help others, even as you enjoy God's gracious provisions? Are you genuinely unselfish, openhanded, greathearted?

I do not know of a more pronounced idol in this generation than "Sir Greed." I'm convinced it is more powerful and certainly more popular than lust. . . . If you are determined to simplify your life, you will need to ask yourself some hard questions: Why do you want that second job? Why are you working such long hours? Why have you deliberately put your family on hold while you play Russian roulette with greed? When will you be able to say, "Enough"?

Simple Faith

How much importance have you placed on material possessions and social status in your life?

_____

_____

_____

GOD BENDS OVER TO LISTEN

I am praying to you because I know you will answer,
O God. Bend down and listen as I pray.
PSALM 17:6

So many of us feel as though we have to hide our failures, believing no one else could possibly have failed as we have. Some are even afraid to tell God about it, fearing He might be as put off as we imagine others will be.

But He isn't like that at all, is He? When we take a tumble and cry out to Him in our shame and our distress, the psalmist says He inclines His ear to us. He bends over to listen. We say, "Oh, Father, I've failed! I've failed terribly. Look at what I've done!" And then He puts His arms around us, just as a loving earthly father would do. He then says, "I accept you just as you are. I acknowledge that what you have done was wrong, as you've confessed it to Me. Now, My son, My daughter, let's move on."

Moses: A Man of Selfless Dedication

Do you truly believe that God bends down to hear you when you pray? If so, why would you ever miss a chance to speak with Him?

_____

_____

_____

_____

THOUGHTS OF EXCELLENCE

We capture their rebellious thoughts and teach them to obey Christ.
2 CORINTHIANS 10:5

The secret of living a life of excellence is merely a matter of thinking thoughts of excellence. Really, it's a matter of programming our minds with the kind of information that will set us free. Free to be all God meant us to be.

Since the mind holds the secrets of soaring, the enemy of our souls has made the human mind the bull's-eye of his target. His most insidious and strategic moves are made upon the mind. By affecting the way we think, he is able to keep our lives on a mediocre level.

God is interested in our breaking free from such locks.

And what is God's ultimate goal? To take "every thought captive" (2 Corinthians 10:5 NASB). When He invades those lofty areas, His plan is to transform the old thoughts that defeat us into new thoughts that encourage us.

Living Above the Level of Mediocrity

Are you monitoring your thoughts and making them conform to the truths of Scripture? Remember, gospel in, gospel out!

_____

_____

_____

FATHER OF MERCIES

*All praise to God, the Father of our Lord Jesus Christ. God
is our merciful Father and the source of all comfort.*
2 CORINTHIANS 1:3

In our world of superficial talk and casual relationships, it's easy to forget that a smile doesn't necessarily mean "I'm happy" and the courteous answer "I'm fine" may not be at all truthful.

I'm not suggesting that everyone is an emotional time bomb or that masks are worn by all who seem to be enjoying life. But I've lived long enough to know that many a heart hides agony while the face reflects ecstasy.

There is Someone, however, who fully knows what lurks in our hearts. And knowing, He never laughs mockingly and fades away. He never shrugs and walks away. Instead, He understands completely and stays near.

He is "our merciful Father and the source of all comfort."

The Finishing Touch

When have you encountered individuals who avoid you in times of suffering? Your heavenly Father draws near.

_____

_____

_____

_____

OUR SHEPHERD LEADS THE WAY

"I am the good shepherd. The good shepherd sacrifices his life for the sheep."
JOHN 10:11

We, as God's sheep, are sometimes led by Him into the valley of darkness, where there is fear, danger, uncertainty, and the unexpected. He knows that the only way we can reach the higher places of Christian experience and maturity is not on the playground of prosperity but in the schoolroom of suffering. Along those dark, narrow, pinching, uncomfortable valleys of difficulty, we learn volumes! We keep our courage simply because our Shepherd is leading the way. Perhaps that is what the writer had in mind when he exhorted us to keep "looking only at Jesus. . . . For consider Him . . . so that you will not grow weary and lose heart" (Hebrews 12:2–3 NASB).

Living Beyond the Daily Grind

Are you trying to find your way out of a valley instead of letting the Shepherd lead you out?

_____

_____

_____

_____

_____

OPEN HANDS, OPEN HEARTS

But if we look forward to something we don't yet have,
we must wait patiently and confidently.
ROMANS 8:25

The word *persevere* is very important. It's an archaic word, and we don't hear much about it in our day of bailing out and giving up. We don't hear much about hanging in there and persevering . . . about staying power! But there is more to it than merely enduring. It's one thing to stand grim-faced, tightfisted, and staring at God with anger, saying, "How *dare you*! What right do You have?" or "Look at what I've done for you! And look at what I get in return!" That's one kind of perseverance. But there's another kind. The kind that stands with an open hand and open arms, that looks into the face of God and replies, "I submit myself to You. I'm trying hard to hear what You're saying. I wholly and completely admit my dependence. I've run out of answers. I'm waiting."

Perfect Trust

Have you come to a place of submission in the midst of suffering, or do you still insist on striving for control?

_____

_____

_____

_____

PROMOTE PEACE

A quarrelsome person starts fights as easily as hot embers light charcoal or fire lights wood.
PROVERBS 26:21

A peacemaker is the servant who . . . first, is at peace with himself—internally, at ease . . . not agitated, ill-tempered, in turmoil . . . and therefore not abrasive. Second, he or she works hard to settle quarrels, not start them . . . is accepting, tolerant, finds no pleasure in being negative.

Ever been around Christians who are *not* peacemakers? Of course. Was it pleasant? Did you sense a servant's heart? Were you built up and encouraged? . . . Was the body of Christ strengthened and supported? You know the answers.

Few things are more godlike than *peace*. When we promote it, pursue it, model it, we are linked directly with Him.

Improving Your Serve

How can you become a better promoter of peace in your home, community, workplace, and church?

GOD DOESN'T DO STANDARD THINGS

The sun has one kind of glory, while the moon and stars each have another kind. And even the stars differ from each other in their glory.
1 CORINTHIANS 15:41

God is not known for doing standard things. He is engaged in doing very distinct things. When a person does something, it has the man or woman look about it. It drips with humanity. You can follow the logic of it and see the meaning behind it. You can even read what they paid for it and how they pulled it off and the organization that made it so slick. God doesn't build skyscrapers; men build skyscrapers. And they all have the touch of genius, human genius. But you cannot find a man who can make a star. And when God steps in, His working is like the difference between a skyscraper and a star.

Perfect Trust

When have you seen God at work and known, without a doubt, that it was Him?

_____

_____

_____

_____

_____

FOCUS FULLY ON GOD

But those who trust in the LORD find new strength.
They will soar high on wings like eagles.
ISAIAH 40:31

We get in a hurry when we don't wait on the Lord. We jump ahead and do rash things. We shoot from the hip. We run off at the mouth, saying things that we later regret. But when we have sufficiently waited on the Lord, He gets full control of our spirit. At such moments, we're like a glove, and His hand is moving us wherever He pleases.

When you wait on the Lord, you don't have to sit in a corner contemplating your navel or walk around in a daze humming "Sweet Hour of Prayer." You don't have to wear a robe and live in a hut in Tibet for the winter. Sometimes, of course, you need to sit down quietly, by yourself, alone with the Lord for a time of quietness. Solitude and silence are wonderful when nourishing our souls. But mostly you go right on with your business. You press on with your regular activities. You just focus more fully on the Lord in the midst of it. You stay preoccupied with Him. You think His thoughts. . . . You feed your soul His manna.

Esther: A Woman of Strength and Dignity

What habits do you have in place that enable you to focus on the Lord consistently throughout your day?

_____

_____

ENDURANCE IS THE SECRET

*"God blesses those who are persecuted for doing right,
for the Kingdom of Heaven is theirs."*
MATTHEW 5:10

Where did Christians get the idea that we'd be appreciated, affirmed, and admired? The Savior Himself taught that blessings are reserved for the persecuted, for those who are reviled, for those against whom folks say all kind of evil . . . falsely (Matthew 5:10–11). It sure is easy to forget those words and get soft, becoming too tender, too sensitive. Fragility is not a virtue extolled in Scripture. Saints with thin skin get distracted and, shortly thereafter, discouraged. There is a long, demanding course to be run, most of which takes place in the trenches and without applause. I suggest we lower our expectations as we intensify our determination and head for the goal.

Endurance is the secret, not popularity.

The Finishing Touch

Have you forgotten that Christians are called, not to a life of ease, but to a life of endurance? How did Jesus describe the life of those who would follow Him?

_____

_____

_____

A STEADY STREAM OF LOVE

I want them to be encouraged and knit together by strong ties of love.
COLOSSIANS 2:2

What is Christ like? He is characterized by love and forgiveness. An insightful person once said, "We are most like beasts when we kill. We are most like men when we judge. We are most like God when we forgive." . . . Every one of us can blame somebody for something that has happened in our lives. But don't waste your time. What we need most is a steady stream of love flowing among us. Love that quickly forgives and willingly overlooks and refuses to take offense.

Some people are so easy to love that you just naturally fall into their arms. But others are so hard to love, you have to work overtime at it. . . . Some are the opposite of magnets. They repel. Yet even they need our love, perhaps more than the others. How very important that we "stretch fervently" to love each other!

Hope Again

Are you knit together with other believers? How have those strong bonds enabled you to endure?

_____

_____

_____

_____

HOLINESS IS PART OF THE PROCESS

"You must consecrate yourselves and be holy, because I am holy."
LEVITICUS 11:44

Some people give the impression that we'll never be able to work hard enough to be holy enough. We'll never give up enough things to be holy. At the opposite extreme are those folks who see holiness as entirely passive. God distributes it. He dumps it on you. You enjoy it, take advantage of it, but you're just a passive part of the process.

Let me correct both of these extremes. First of all, we must be holy. Holiness always suggests . . . separateness and difference. God, being holy, is different and separate from all other gods. And we, as His children, must be separate and different as well. . . . We must live lives of ethical integrity and moral excellence. If that were impossible for us, God would never require it of us. But He does.

Second, holiness is not passive. It isn't all up to God. We are active participants in the process. Holiness is part of the process of the will of God for us, His children.

The Mystery of God's Will

How are you seeking to live a holy life that imitates God?

_____

_____

_____

LOVE YOURSELF, LOVE YOUR WIFE

In the same way, husbands ought to love their
wives as they love their own bodies.
EPHESIANS 5:28

Let that verse sink in, men. The love we are to demonstrate on behalf of our wives is in direct proportion to the love we have for ourselves—not a noisy conceit, but a quiet and deep sense of self-worth. Show me a wife who feels loved and appreciated by her husband, and I'll guarantee she is married to a man who properly loves himself. But if she's a wife who sighs and says, "Couldn't somebody teach my husband how to love me!" I can assure you she has a man whose self-esteem is lagging.

Until you have a proper sense of self-love, a healthy and wholesome self-esteem, you are not able to freely and fully love someone else. You don't give yourself to others or consider them valuable if you don't first of all consider yourself worthy. . . . Love draws upon the resourcefulness of one's own esteem in order to have sufficient supply to release it to someone else. It takes personal security to do that.

Growing Wise in Family Life

Do you grasp how much you are loved by God? How does grasping this truth affect your ability to love others?

_____

_____

SWEETER THAN HONEY

How sweet your words taste to me; they are sweeter than honey.
PSALM 119:103

Back before the collapse of the atheistic Soviet Union, my friend John Van Diest represented the Evangelical Christian Publishers Association at the Moscow Book Fair. The authorities had granted them reluctant permission to hand out a limited number of Russian language New Testaments, and long lines of people waited to receive a copy. When the supplies were exhausted, one desperately disappointed man asked if he might have one of the empty boxes that had once held those Testaments.

"But there's nothing in there!" John protested. "The Bibles are all gone!" With tears glistening in his eyes, the man replied, "Then I at least want the box." The Bible was so precious to this man that he treasured the cardboard box that had held the Scriptures. May our eyes be opened to the astonishing privilege that is ours to hold the complete written Word of God in our very hands.

Moses: A Man of Selfless Dedication

How can you better cherish the Word of God in your life?

_____

_____

_____

_____

THE GODLY TAKE GOD SERIOUSLY

As the deer longs for streams of water, so I long for you, O God.
PSALM 42:1

Whatever we may say godliness is, it is *not* skin deep. It is something below the surface of a life, deep down in the realm of an attitude . . . an attitude toward God Himself.

The longer I think about this, the more I believe that a person who is godly is one whose heart is sensitive toward God, one who takes God seriously. This evidences itself in one very obvious mannerism: the godly individual hungers and thirsts after God. In the words of the psalmist, the godly person has a soul that "pants" for the living God (Psalm 42:1 NASB).

The one who sustains this pursuit may be young or old, rich or poor, urban or rural, leader or follower, of any race or color or culture or any temperament, active or quiet, married or single; none of these things really matter. But what does matter is the individual's inner craving to know God, listen to Him, and walk humbly with Him. As I mentioned, the godly take Him seriously.

Strengthening Your Grip

How can you better sustain your pursuit of the living God?

_____

_____

_____

AN ENDLESS CYCLE

Everything is wearisome beyond description. No matter how much we see,
we are never satisfied. No matter how much we hear, we are not content.
ECCLESIASTES 1:8

You work so that you can make money, so that you can spend it, so that you can work and make more money, so that you can spend it, so that you can get more, which will mean you spend more, and you'll work harder to make more. So goes this endless cycle.

That explains why people will line up by the millions to view a fantasy on film and sit in silent amazement at someone's imaginary world of imaginary characters who do imaginary things—because life under the sun is so dreadfully, unchangingly boring.

To put it bluntly, life on planet Earth *without* God is the pits. That's the way God designed it. He made it like that. He placed within us that God-shaped vacuum that only He can fill. Until He is there, nothing satisfies. There is no hell on earth like horizontal living without God.

Living on the Ragged Edge

Do you find yourself going through each day wondering about the point of it all? How does God improve your perspective?

_____

_____

_____

You're in Good Hands

Yes, praise the LORD, you armies of angels who serve him and do his will!
PSALM 103:21

What does it mean to say that God is faithful? It means He is steadfast in His allegiance to His people. He will not leave us in the lurch. It also means He is firm in his adherence to His promises. He keeps His word. Faithfulness suggests the idea of loyalty: dependability; constancy; being resolute, steady, and consistent. God isn't fickle; no hot-and-cold temperamental moods with Him!

God is also faithful to remember His servants.

He remembers our work—each individual act.

He takes note of the love within us that prompted the deed.

No one on earth can do those special things. We forget, but God remembers. We see the action; God sees the motive. This qualifies Him as the best record keeper and judge. He alone is perfectly and consistently just. You're in good hands with the Almighty!

Improving Your Serve

Do you need a reminder that God sees all? That nothing you do in His name or out of love for others is overlooked?

_____

_____

_____

GOD RENOVATES OUR SOULS

But you desire honesty from the womb, teaching me wisdom even there.
PSALM 51:6

God must break through several hard, exterior barriers in our lives before He can renovate our souls. His persistent goal is to break through to the inner person.

What are those resistant layers in our hearts, and how does He break through to that *hidden part?* First, He finds pride. And He uses the sandpaper of obscurity to remove it ever so gradually.

Then He finds us gripped by fear—dread of our past, anxiety over our present, and terror over what may lie ahead—and He uses the passing of time to remove that fear. We learn that things aren't out of hand at all; they're in His hand.

He next encounters the barrier of resentment—the tyranny of bitterness. He breaks down that layer with solitude. In the silence of His presence, we gain a fresh perspective, gradually release our cherished *rights,* and let go of the expectations that held us hostage.

Moses: A Man of Selfless Dedication

Do you still see yourself through the lens of your failures and fears, or are you enjoying the freedom of a renovated soul?

_____

_____

HONEST-TO-GOODNESS MEN

Whoever pursues righteousness and unfailing love
will find life, righteousness, and honor.
PROVERBS 21:21

I'm concerned about a vanishing masculinity that was once in abundance. I mean honest-to-goodness men who are distinctly that—discerning, decisive, strong-hearted men who know where they are going and are confident enough in themselves (and their God) to get there. They aren't afraid to take the lead, to stand tall and firm in their principles even when the going gets rough.

Such qualities not only inspire the respect of women, but they also engender healthy admiration among younger men and boys who hunger for heroes. We need . . . more clear-thinking, hardworking, straight-talking men who, while tender, thoughtful, and loving, don't feel the need to ask permission for taking charge. I'm convinced that most single ladies would love to have men like that to spend time with . . . and most wives long to have men like that to share life with. Children especially like having dads like that.

Growing Wise in Family Life

Are you confident in your God-given role as a man? Do you allow the men in your life to live out God's design for them?

_____

_____

_____

345

HEARTS THAT ARE HIS

My child, if your heart is wise, my own heart will rejoice!
Everything in me will celebrate when you speak what is right.
PROVERBS 23:15–16

When God's call comes, will He find us ready and willing to stand for Him? Will He find in us hearts that are completely His? Will He be able to say, "Ah, yes, that one's heart is completely Mine. Yes, there's sufficient commitment there for Me to use that life"?

If your Christianity hasn't put that kind of steel in your spine, that quality of marrow in your bones, there's something terribly wrong, either with the message you're hearing or with your heart. God is looking for men and women whose hearts are completely His, men and women who won't blend into the scenery.

What spot has God given you? Whatever it is, God says, "You're standing before *Me*, and I want to use you. I want to use you as My unique spokesperson in your day and age, at this moment and time."

Elijah: A Man of Heroism & Humility

Are you willing to stand boldly for Christ and to be used in a way that will make it clear where your loyalties lie?

_____

_____

_____

INTEGRITY AND HONESTY

He grants a treasure of common sense to the honest. He is a shield to those who walk with integrity. He guards the paths of the just and protects those who are faithful to him.

PROVERBS 2:7–8

I f we walk in integrity, we will not stumble. What a great thought! If we decide that we will live honestly—which means, for example, conducting an honest business—we will not stumble into dishonesty. We will model honesty. God promises He will honor that. He will protect us. That means that ultimately we win over the ungodly. We gain because we're living in the realm of honesty and they're not. He stores up sound wisdom for us. With it, He gives us a shield of protection as we walk in integrity.

God is ready to do His part whenever we're ready to do ours.

Living on the Ragged Edge

When have you acted in integrity and found the Lord guarding you just as He promised?

_____

_____

_____

_____

_____

WALKING BY FAITH

We stopped relying on ourselves and learned to rely only on God. . . . We have placed our confidence in him, and he will continue to rescue us.
2 CORINTHIANS 1:9–10

The old motto of soldiers during the Revolutionary War applies to many areas of life: "Trust in God, but keep your powder dry!" In other words, place your life in the Savior's hands, but stay at the ready. Do all that you can to prepare yourself for battle, understanding that the ultimate outcome rests with the Lord God.

To walk by faith does not mean to stop *thinking*. To trust God does not imply becoming slovenly or lazy or apathetic. . . . You and I need to trust God for our finances, but that is no license to spend foolishly. You and I ought to trust God for safety in the car, but we're not wise to pass on a blind curve.

Acting foolishly or thoughtlessly, expecting God to bail you out if things go amiss, isn't faith at all. It is presumption. Wisdom says do all you can within your strength, then trust Him to do what you cannot do.

Moses: A Man of Selfless Dedication

In what areas of your life do you need to stop relying on yourself and begin relying only on God?

_____

_____

_____

SET YOURSELF APART

But now you must be holy in everything you do,
just as God who chose you is holy.
1 PETER 1:15

What does it mean to be *holy?* . . . Stripped down to its basics, the term *holy* means "set apart" in some special and exclusive way. . . . In holy matrimony, for example, a man and a woman are set apart, leaving all others as they bond exclusively to each other.

In Holy Communion . . . the bread and wine are set apart from common use and set aside to God alone. The same meaning lies behind the word *sanctify* in 1 Peter 3:15: "But sanctify Christ as Lord in your hearts" (NASB). . . . We are to "set Him apart" as Lord in our hearts.

What a successful way to deal with the cosmos! To begin the morning by saying, "Lord, I set apart my mind for You today. . . . I set apart every limb of my body and each area of my life unto You as Lord over my life." When we start our day like that, chances are good that temptation's wink will not be nearly as alluring.

Hope Again

What if you set apart everything for God's glory today: your health, wealth, sufferings, and successes?

_____

_____

Free to Fly

All praise to God, the Father of our Lord Jesus Christ. It is by his great mercy that we have been born again, because God raised Jesus Christ from the dead.
1 Peter 1:3

Grace frees us to fly. So, fly! Dare I give a few illustrations? Aw, why not? You've had your eyes on that sailboat or catamaran or sports car for some time. Why not? You've thought a lot about a cruise or a trip to Europe but never permitted yourself to do more than think. Why not?

Your hairdo has looked the same for three decades. You've wondered about trying something really *chic*. Why not?

You long to get your degree, but everybody tells you to give up that dream. Should you press on? Why not?

You'd love to throw a big, crazy party with a few happy-go-lucky folks who know how to have fun. Why in the world not?

Grace frees us to fly. So, fly!

Day by Day with Charles Swindoll

In His presence is fullness of joy! What would it look like for you to live in the freedom of that joy each day?

_____

_____

_____

DECEMBER

SHAPED BY GOD

So all of us . . . can see and reflect the glory of the Lord.
2 CORINTHIANS 3:18

A sculptor was asked how he could carve a lion's head out of a large block of marble. "I just chip away everything that doesn't look like a lion's head," was his reply. God works away in our being and chips away everything that doesn't look like Christ—the impatience, the short temper, the pride, the emotional drives that lead us away from our Father. He's shaping us into His image. That's His predetermined plan. And He's committed to it. Nothing we can do will dissuade Him from that plan. He stays at it. He is relentless. And He never runs out of creative ideas.

That's why he sends one person to the mission field in China and another to the bank building in downtown Seattle. That's part of His sovereign plan to shape individuals into the image of Christ.

The Mystery of God's Will

How are you reflecting the glory of Christ in the places where God has placed you today?

_____

_____

_____

_____

INFECTIOUS JOY

We were filled with laughter, and we sang for joy. And the other nations said, "What amazing things the LORD has done for them."

PSALM 126:2

Perhaps you find yourself among those in the if-only group. You say you would laugh *if only* you had more money . . . *if only* you had more talent or were more beautiful . . . *if only* you could find a more fulfilling job. I challenge those excuses. Just as more money never made anyone generous and more talent never made anyone grateful, more of *anything* never made anyone joyful.

Without exception, people who consistently laugh do so *in spite of,* seldom *because of* anything. They pursue fun rather than wait for it to knock on their door in the middle of the day. Such infectiously joyful believers have no trouble convincing people around them that Christianity is real and that Christ can transform a life. Joy is the flag that flies above the castle of their hearts, announcing that the King is in residence.

Laugh Again

Would others know, by the joy in your life, that the Lord has done amazing things for you?

DEPENDING WHOLLY ON GOD

*"God blesses those who are poor and realize their need
for him, for the Kingdom of Heaven is theirs."*
MATTHEW 5:3

Blessed are the poor in spirit" (Matthew 5:3 NASB). Not poor in substance, but spirit. This first beatitude has nothing to do with being materially destitute or financially bankrupt. Jesus is placing value on a humble spirit, on those who acknowledge a spiritual bankruptcy in and of themselves. Where there is an absence of well-polished pride and personal conceit, there is a wholesome dependence on the living God. Instead of, "No problem, I can handle it. . . . " there is a quick confession, acknowledging one's own inadequacies.

And the promised blessing for such a humble, dependent . . . attitude? "Theirs is the kingdom of heaven" (NASB). By living lives of such *Simple Faith* beneath our Father's sovereign, gracious care, we truly enter into what kingdom living is all about.

Simple Faith

Have you set aside your pride and embraced the life of the poor in spirit? Why is that way better?

_____

_____

_____

GETTING ACQUAINTED WITH CHRIST

*I want to know Christ and experience the mighty power that raised
him from the dead. I want to suffer with him, sharing in his death.*
PHILIPPIANS 3:10

Like the great apostle Paul, let's make this our "determined purpose" (Philippians 3:10 AMPC). Let's deliberately embrace this aim: to "become more . . . intimately acquainted with Him" (AMPC). Not intimately acquainted with theology, as important as theology may be. Not intimately acquainted with the church, as valuable as the church may be. Not with sharing Christ with others, as stimulating and significant as evangelism may be. No, none of the above!

With Christ. With Him and Him alone! From this time forward, our goal in life is to become intimately acquainted with Him. I believe this is precisely what Jesus had in mind when He commanded, "Seek first the kingdom of God and His righteousness" (Matthew 6:33 NKJV).

There is nothing—absolutely nothing—of greater importance than knowing Christ intensely and intimately.

Intimacy with the Almighty

How are you being intentional about knowing Christ more intimately each day?

_____

_____

S KIMMING THE T REETOPS

For he knows how weak we are; he remembers we are only dust.
P SALM 103:14

G od is mindful that He created us as finite beings out of a few pounds of garden soil. He understands that. . . . My question is, why don't we under-stand it? Why do we expect perfection of ourselves and of our associates?

You and I become terribly impatient with our own shortcomings and lim-itations and with each other. We despair because we think we ought to be in spiritual orbit by this time, when we're barely skimming the treetops. . . . We think we ought instantly, constantly, and effectively to conquer vast territories for the kingdom, like some spiritual Alexander the Great. And when it doesn't happen—when victory seems elusive—we grow discouraged.

Whenever I start feeling like that, I need to revisit the life of Moses. . . . Here was a man who didn't become effective for God until he was *eighty*. Long after most of us would be riding a rocking chair or pushing up daisies, Moses began his spiritual career. And guess what? God used him mightily.

Moses: A Man of Selfless Dedication

Are you too hard on yourself? Do you expect more from yourself than the God who created you?

_____

_____

_____

GOD'S APPLAUSE

I could have no greater joy than to hear that my children are following the truth.

3 JOHN v. 4

Great word, *enthusiasm*. Its Greek origin is *entheos,* "God in." It is the ability to see God in a situation that makes it exciting. Do you know that God is watching your life? Do you realize that? Something happens to us when we become convinced that God our heavenly Father is aware of and involved in our activities and is, in fact, applauding our lives.

Think of all you have accomplished to this point. Try to imagine the horizons and challenges of your future. As you mentally travel from the vanishing point of yesterday to the vanishing point of tomorrow, you will find that God has been and always will be present. There is not a place in the entire scope of your existence where God is not there.

Living Above the Level of Mediocrity

How do you feel knowing that God is completely invested in you and interested in all that you do?

_____

_____

_____

_____

_____

PREFER GIVING

"It is more blessed to give than to receive."
ACTS 20:35

Yourself, yourself, yourself. We're up to here with self! Do something either *for* yourself or *with* yourself or *to* yourself. How very different from Jesus' model and message! No "philosophy" to turn our eyes inward, He offers rather a fresh and much-needed invitation to our "me-first" generation. There is a better way. Jesus says, "Be a servant. Give to others!" Now that's a philosophy that anybody can understand. And without question, it is attainable.

Stop permitting two strong tendencies—selfishness and conceit—to control you! Let nothing either of them suggests win a hearing. Replace them with "humility of mind." How? By regarding others as more important than yourself. Look for ways to support, encourage, build up, and stimulate the other person. And that requires an attitude that would rather give than receive.

Improving Your Serve

Do you find yourself too inwardly focused? In what ways can you give to someone else today?

_____

_____

_____

_____

EMMANUEL—GOD WITH US

Don't be afraid! . . . I bring you good news that will bring great
joy to all people. The Savior—yes, the Messiah, the Lord—
has been born today in Bethlehem, the city of David!
LUKE 2:10–11

Christmas comes each year to draw people in from the cold.
Like tiny, frightened sparrows, shivering in the winter cold, many live
their lives on the barren branches of heartbreak, disappointment, and loneliness, lost in thoughts of shame, self-pity, guilt, or failure.

Then, as the year draws to a close, Christmas offers its wonderful message.
Emmanuel. God with us. He who resided in heaven, co-equal and co-eternal
with the Father and the Spirit, willingly descended into our world. He breathed
our air, felt our pain, knew our sorrows, and died for our sins. He didn't come
to frighten us, but to show us the way to warmth and safety.

The Finishing Touch

How does the presence of God in your life enable you to withstand the
often harsh and cold conditions of the world?

_____

_____

_____

_____

A Dash of Panic

Trust in the Lord with all your heart; do not depend on your own understanding.
Proverbs 3:5

A gentleman in our church was injured on a ski outing and as a result was confined to crutches for many long weeks. Sometimes you would find him panting at the top of a flight of stairs. If you looked at his hands, you would notice they had gotten red and sore. He truly found that leaning on crutches was *exhausting*.

So is leaning on our own understanding! If you want to spend an exhausting day, try to work out your circumstances leaning on your *human viewpoint*. Chase down all the possibilities you can think of. When you hit a dead-end street, back out, then turn down into another one. Drive fast, then slam on your brakes. Throw in a dash of panic, a pinch of fear, add a tablespoon of manipulation, three cups of scheming, and a handful of pills! When you are through, consider where you have been. That is an excellent recipe for "instant depression." Furthermore, you will be mentally exhausted. Peace will flee from you.

Living Beyond the Daily Grind

Have you exhausted yourself leaning on all the wrong things for support? Why not lean completely on the Lord today?

_____

_____

A GALLERY OF MEMORIES

My God! Now I am deeply discouraged, but I will remember you.
PSALM 42:6

Our past is like an art gallery. Walking down those corridors of our memory is like walking through an art gallery. On the walls are all of yesterday's pictures: our home, our childhood, our parents, our rearing, the heartaches, the difficulties, the joys and triumphs as well as the abuses and the inequities of our life. Since Jesus Christ our Lord is the same yesterday and today and forever, then we can take the Christ of today and walk with Him into our yesterday and ask Him to remove the pictures that bring bad or defeating memories. In other words, the Christian can let Jesus invade yesterday and deal with those years of affliction—those years which the locusts have eaten (Joel 2:25–26)—and remove those scenes from the corridors of our lives. I have them. You have them. We need to let Him leave the murals that bring pleasure and victory and take down from the walls those things that bring despair and defeat.

David: A Man of Passion and Destiny

How does dwelling on the goodness of God help you overcome the temptation to be discouraged?

_____

_____

_____

ASK GOD TO TAKE CHARGE

We can rejoice, too, when we run into problems and trials,
for we know that they help us develop endurance.
ROMANS 5:3

O ne of the Greek terms for *tribulation* in the New Testament refers to "pressure . . . like being crushed under a big boulder." This is a description of pain, of enduring strain. It's an illustration of the crush of our times. There's a certain kind of pressure that comes with unemployment. There's another kind of pressure that comes with the threat of losing your home. There's a pressure that comes from calamity or a wayward child or a runaway mate.

Does God care about the number of hairs on your scalp? Does He care if a sparrow falls? Yes, His Word assures us He does. Then be assured of this: He's a specialist in the things that worry you down inside. The things you dread tomorrow or this coming week. The things that make you wonder, *How can I get this together?* God's reassurance to you is, "Look, that's what I specialize in. I can take that situation you've built into a mountain, and I can bore a tunnel through it in a matter of seconds. Bring all of it to Me. Ask Me to take charge."

Perfect Trust

Do you believe that God cares about and is capable of handling all of your worries—big or small?

_____

_____

REMEMBER THE RIGHT, FORGET THE WRONG

The reward of the godly will last. Godly people find life.
PROVERBS 11:18–19

Whether a personal or public matter, we quickly reveal whether we possess a servant's heart in how we respond to those who have offended us. And it isn't enough simply to say, "Well, okay—you're forgiven, but don't expect me to forget it!" That means we have erected a monument of spite in our mind, and that isn't really forgiveness at all. Servants must be big people. Big enough to *go on,* remembering the right and forgetting the wrong. Like the age-old saying, "Write injuries in dust, benefits in marble."

True servants, when demonstrating genuine love, don't keep score. Merriam-Webster defines *forget* as "to lose the remembrance of . . . to treat with inattention or disregard . . . to disregard intentionally: overlook . . . to cease remembering or noticing . . . to fail to become mindful at the proper time." That's the thought.

Improving Your Serve

Is there an offense that you need to overlook? How does this willingness to forgive make you more like Christ?

_____

_____

_____

GOD'S PRESENCE AND POWER

I trust in God, so why should I be afraid? What can mere mortals do to me?
PSALM 56:4

We take a look at the money in our pockets, and it says, "In God we trust." Trust Him to do what? Keep us free from invasion? Make us prosperous? Sustain our position of world power and leadership? Yet as a nation today we are much more self-reliant . . . than we are God-reliant.

Here's a direct question: "Can you trust God?" There are two ways to look at that question. Can you *trust* God? That is, is He dependable in times of need? Will He do what He says? Or secondly, we might ask, "Can *you* trust God? Do *you* have such a relationship with Him and such confidence in Him that you believe He is with you always even though you do not see any evidence of His presence and His power?

Perfect Trust

How has God proven Himself trustworthy in your life? Are you trusting Him with the current battle you face?

_____

_____

_____

_____

JUST SAY, "NO!"

Take my words to heart. Follow my commands, and you will live.

Joseph was a good-looking man who, without interest in doing so, caught the eye of a woman (Genesis 39:6–7).

Potiphar's wife was brazenly and shamelessly aggressive [toward him]: "Come to bed with me. Let's have sex." Most others then and now would have been caught off guard and at least momentarily felt flattered. . . . Not Joseph. Not even for a moment. Without hesitation and being absolutely secure in himself and his God, he responded with equal boldness.

He refused! . . . Don't forget those two wonderful words. Here was an Egyptian woman offering her body and a young Jewish servant being tempted by her bold advance. And so? He refused. He said no!

How could he do that? Two reasons—his loyalty to his master, Potiphar . . . and his loyalty to God (v. 9).

Joseph: A Man of Integrity and Forgiveness

Are you toying with temptation in some area of life? How can you remove yourself from the situation?

EVERYONE IS INCLUDED

And let the peace that comes from Christ rule in your hearts. For as members of one body you are called to live in peace. And always be thankful.
COLOSSIANS 3:15

When the world looks for qualities that will get the job done, the externals get the nod. We like people with charisma, people who have pizzazz, who can put up a good front. I've noticed in the past twenty-plus years, we are looking less and less for integrity and honor and true character in a president. We look for people who look good on television, people who can debate an opponent with great ease and little facial sweat, who can compromise enough to please just about everyone. We prefer the externals. Character we'll do without if we have to, but not those externals. But God passes up the externals and looks for the humble of heart!

We live in a world where we take care of our own. We look out for number one. But God's plan encompasses everyone. Every nation. Every race. All cultures. Huge, highly developed countries, but not excluding the small, struggling ones. His message of *shalom* (peace) through faith in Christ is universal. Unlimited. Without prejudice. Vast!

Esther: A Woman of Strength and Dignity

When have you been drawn to a person because of external qualities only to be disappointed in their internal character?

_____

_____

MAKE A DIFFERENCE

*What good is it, dear brothers and sisters, if you say you
have faith but don't show it by your actions?*
JAMES 2:14

Does one person make a difference? Let me ask you, did Christ? God so loved the world that He *did something*. He didn't select a committee. He didn't theorize how great it would be for someone to come to our rescue. He didn't simply grieve over our waywardness and wring His hands in sorrow. He did something! And, in turn, the Son of God said to God the Father, "I will go." He *did something* about it. And that's why we can be saved. We don't believe in a theory; we believe in the person of Christ, who died and rose again that we might live and make a difference.

The question is not simply, what do you think of Christ? The question is, what have you done about what you think?

Esther: A Woman of Strength and Dignity

How do the things you believe make a difference in how you live day to day?

_____

_____

_____

_____

_____

NO SHORTCUTS

Oh, the joys of those who do not follow the advice of the wicked. . . . But they delight in the law of the LORD.
PSALM 1:1–2

Years ago I read of the construction of a city hall and fire station in a small Pennsylvania community. The citizens were so proud of their new red brick structure—a long-awaited dream come true. Not too many weeks after moving in, however, strange things began to happen. Several doors failed to shut completely, and a few windows wouldn't slide open very easily. As time passed, ominous cracks began to appear in the walls. Within a few months, the front door couldn't be locked . . . and the roof began to leak. By and by, the little building that was once the source of great pride had to be condemned. An intense investigation revealed that deep mining blasts several miles away caused underground shock waves that subsequently weakened the earth beneath the building foundation, resulting in its virtual self-destruction.

So it is with compromise in a life. Slowly, almost imperceptibly, one rationalization leads to another, which triggers a series of equally damaging alterations in a life that was once stable, strong, and reliable.

Living Beyond the Daily Grind

What specific shockwaves from the world have you had to stand against lately? How has Christ's foundation strengthened you?

_____

_____

EXPECT THE UNEXPECTED

Praise the LORD God, the God of Israel, who alone does such wonderful things.
PSALM 72:18

When it came time for God to send His Son to earth, He did not send Him to the palace of some mighty king. He was conceived in the womb of an unwed mother—a virgin!—who lived in the lowly village of Nazareth.

In choosing those who would represent Christ and establish His church, God picked some of the most unusual individuals imaginable: unschooled fishermen, a tax collector (!), a mystic, a doubter, and a former Pharisee who had persecuted Christians. He continued to pick some very unusual persons down through the ages. In fact, He seems to delight in such surprising choices to this very day.

So, let God be God. Expect the unexpected.

The Finishing Touch

What surprising people has God placed in your path over the years? What unexpected ways has He worked in your life?

_____

_____

_____

_____

_____

THE GOAL IS HOPE

Faith shows the reality of what we hope for; it is
the evidence of things we cannot see.
HEBREWS 11:1

Can you remember a recent "gray slush" day? Of course you can. So can I. The laws of fairness and justice were displaced by a couple of Murphy's Laws. Your dream dissolved into a nightmare. High hopes took a hike. Good intentions got lost in a comedy of errors; only this time nobody was laughing. . . . You felt like telling Bunyan to move over as you slid down into his Slough of Despond near Doubting Castle.

Discouragement may be awful, but it is not terminal.

God has an ultimate goal in mind: that we might have hope. And what leads to such a goal? Two things: perseverance and encouragement from the Scriptures. Again, the goal is hope. God has not designed a life of despondency for us. He wants His people to have hope . . . through endurance and through encouragement from the Scriptures.

Living Above the Level of Mediocrity

When you study Scripture, what are some things you don't yet see but believe are coming?

_____

_____

ONE DAY AT A TIME

Pride leads to disgrace, but with humility comes wisdom.
PROVERBS 11:2

People who refuse to get bogged down in and anchored to the past are those who pursue the objectives of the future. People who do this are seldom petty. They are too involved in getting a job done to be occupied with yesterday's hurts and concerns.

I know human nature well enough to realize that some people excuse their bitterness over past hurts by thinking, *It's too late to change. I've been injured, and the wrong done against me is too great for me ever to forget it.*

But when God holds out hope, when God makes promises, when God says, "It can be done," there are *no exceptions*. With each new dawn there is delivered to your door a fresh, new package called "today." God has designed us in such a way that we can handle only one package at a time . . . and all the grace we need will be supplied by Him as we live out that day.

Improving Your Serve

Do you find yourself making excuses for your bitterness? Why not choose to let yesterday go?

_____

_____

_____

MARVELS AND MYSTERIES OF THE DEEP

For his Spirit searches out everything and shows us God's deep secrets.
1 CORINTHIANS 2:10

Deep things are intriguing. Deep jungles. Deep water. Deep caves and canyons. Deep thoughts and conversations.

There is nothing like depth to make us dissatisfied with superficial, shallow things. Once we have delved below the surface and had a taste of the marvels and mysteries of the deep, we realize the value of taking the time and going to the trouble of plumbing those depths.

This is especially true in the spiritual realm. God invites us to go deeper rather than to be content with surface matters.

Intimacy with the Almighty

Do you have an insatiable desire to go deeper with God? If not, why not ask Him to give it to you today?

_____

_____

_____

_____

_____

_____

RELIEF INSTEAD OF REVENGE

Sensible people control their temper; they earn respect by overlooking wrongs.
PROVERBS 19:11

Are you aware of the joy-stealing effect an unforgiving spirit is having on your life? If your bitterness is deep enough, you've virtually stopped living.

It's not worth it. You need to come to terms with this lingering, nagging issue now. The peace and contentment and joy that could be yours are draining away, like water down the drain of an unplugged bathtub. It's time for you to call a halt to the dispute: the disharmony must be defused.

Start by telling God how much it hurts and that you need Him to help you to forgive the offense. . . . Get rid of all the poison of built-up anger and pour out all the acid of long-term resentment. Your objective is clear: fully forgive the offender. Once that is done, you will discover that you no longer rehearse the ugly scenes in your mind. The revengeful desire to get back and get even will wane, and in its now-empty space will come such an outpouring of relief and a new spirit of joy that you won't feel like the same person.

Laugh Again

What is holding you back from forgiving someone? How has that unforgiveness held you back from a joyful life?

_____

_____

_____

THE SCHOOLROOM OF LIFE

Examine yourselves to see if your faith is genuine. Test yourselves.
2 CORINTHIANS 13:5

Life is a schoolroom. In it, we encounter pop quizzes and periodic examinations. You can't have a schoolroom without tests—at least I've never seen one. . . . Throughout the educational process our knowledge is assessed on the basis of examinations. The curriculum of Christlikeness is much the same. Our Christian maturity is measured by our ability to withstand the tests that come our way without having them shake our foundation or throw us into an emotional or spiritual tailspin.

The wonderful thing about God's schoolroom, however, is that we get to grade our own papers. You see, He doesn't test us so He can learn how well we're doing. He tests us so *we* can discover how well we're doing.

Hope Again

How are you handling your current test? Has your faith been apparent?

_____

_____

_____

_____

_____

THE ETERNAL I AM

We do this by keeping our eyes on Jesus, the champion who initiates and perfects our faith.

HEBREWS 12:2

U ntil your eyes are fixed on the Lord, you will not be able to endure those days that go from bad to worse.

Fix your eyes on the Lord! Do it once. Do it daily. Do it ten thousand times ten thousand times. Do it constantly. When your schedule presses, when your prospects thin, when your hope burns low, when people disappoint you, when events turn against you, when dreams die, when the walls close in, when the prognosis seems grim, when your heart breaks, *look at the Lord, and keep on looking at Him.*

Who is He? He is Yahweh, the eternal I AM, the sovereign Lord of the universe. He cannot do what is unjust; it is against His nature. He has never lost control. He is always faithful. Changeless. All-powerful. All-knowing. Good. Compassionate. Gracious. Wise. Loving. Sovereign. Reliable.

Moses: A Man of Selfless Dedication

How are you able to keep your eyes fixed on Jesus throughout your day?

_____

_____

_____

THINK DIFFERENTLY

The way of the godly leads to life; that path does not lead to death.
PROVERBS 12:28

S top being squeezed in! Quit aping the system of thought that surrounds
you, its line of reasoning, its method of operation, its style and techniques!
How? By a radical transformation within. By a renewed thought pattern that
demonstrates authentic godlikeness. Living differently begins with thinking
differently. A life that is characterized by serving others begins in a mind that
is convinced of such a life. That explains why that great section of Scripture
describing Christ's willingness to take upon Himself the form of a servant
begins with the words: "Let this mind be in you, which was also in Christ Jesus"
(Philippians 2:5 KJV).

Jesus' life of serving was the outworking of His mind—"Unsqueezed" by the
world system in all its selfishness—and remains, forever, our example to follow.

Improving Your Serve

How do you develop the mind of Christ? How does such a mindset
manifest itself in your life?

_____

_____

_____

_____

GOD'S ULTIMATE DESIGN

But when hard times strike, realize that both come from God.
ECCLESIASTES 7:14

The Lord God is just as involved and caring during adversity as during prosperity. The Hebrew term translated "consider" suggests the idea "to examine for the purpose of evaluating." In the hard times—when the bottom drops out, enduring days of financial reversal, or severe domestic conflicts—wisdom allows us to examine, to evaluate with incredible objectivity.

God wants us to walk by faith, not by sight.... His ultimate design is nothing short of perfect. He's got a plan, but without operating on the basis of His wisdom, we'll panic and run, or we'll stubbornly resist His way.

Living on the Ragged Edge

How does knowing that God is as equally involved in bad times as He is in good times help you endure the difficult days?

_____

_____

_____

_____

_____

_____

MIMIC GOD

Don't envy sinners, but always continue to fear the LORD.
PROVERBS 23:17

S ince most humans suffer from a lack of balance in their lives, our best counsel on this subject comes from God's Word, the Bible. In that Book, there
appears a most unusual command: "Follow God's example, therefore, as dearly
loved children" (Ephesians 5:1 NIV). Maybe you never realized such a statement
was in the Bible. What a strange command: "Be imitators of God" (NASB)!

In other words, this is neither a passing thought nor a once-in-a-blue-moon
experience. The practice of our being people who mimic God is to become our
daily habit. We are to do what He does. Respond to life as He responds. Emulate
similar traits. Model His style.

Strengthening Your Grip

How are you imitating God in your attitudes and actions on a day-to-day
basis?

_____

_____

_____

_____

_____

SHARING FREELY

But if we are living in the light, as God is in the light, then we have fellowship with each other, and the blood of Jesus, his Son, cleanses us from all sin.

1 JOHN 1:7

Ancient *koinonia* (fellowship) must have been something to behold. As I try to form a mental picture of it, I come up with this description: *Koinonia* is expressions of authentic Christianity freely shared among members of God's family. It is mentioned about twenty times in the New Testament, and without exception it is invariably expressed in one of two directions.

First, it is used in the sense of sharing something *with* someone, such as food, money, supplies, encouragement, time, and concern. And second, it is used in the sense of sharing *in* something with someone, like a project, a success, a failure, a need, a hurt.

The significance of all this is that biblical *koinonia* is *never something done alone.* In other words, God's desire for His children is that we be personally and deeply involved in each other's lives. . . . Our superficial "How ya' doin'" and "Have a nice day" won't cut it.

Strengthening Your Grip

Are you currently living in deep fellowship with other believers, or do you suffer from superficial relationships?

_____

_____

A SERVANT'S HEART

So look at Apollos and me as mere servants of Christ who
have been put in charge of explaining God's mysteries.
1 CORINTHIANS 4:1

A spirit of humility is very rare in our day of strong-willed, proud-as-a-peacock attitudes. The clenched fist has replaced the bowed head. The big mouth and the surly stare now dominate the scene once occupied by the quiet godliness of the "poor in spirit." How self-righteous we have become! How confident in and of ourselves! And with that attitude, how desperately unhappy we are! Christ Jesus offers genuine, lasting happiness to those whose hearts willingly declare:

> *Nothing in my hand I bring, simply to Thy cross I cling.*
> —AUGUSTUS M. TOPLADY

The indispensable condition of receiving a part in the kingdom of heaven is acknowledging our spiritual poverty. The person with a servant's heart—not unlike a child trusting completely in his parent's provision—is promised a place in Christ's kingdom.

Improving Your Serve

What does it look like for you to live humbly in the moment and, at the same time, confidently that God will reward your service in heaven?

_____

_____

DO WHAT IS RIGHT

So let us come boldly to the throne of our gracious God. There we will receive his mercy, and we will find grace to help us when we need it most.

HEBREWS 4:16

Every day we live, we have a choice to do what is right or what is wrong. When we send our young children off to school, we tell them, "Now, sweetheart, you need to know that Mom and Dad won't be there to make your decisions. You will find some kids at school who will encourage you to do what is right and you'll find others who will lead you to disobey and do what is wrong. Make the right choice. Select your friends carefully. Be smart."

Before Christ, we had no choice. Sin was our one and only route. All of life was marked by unrighteousness. But once we came to the cross and gave the Lord Jesus the right to rule our lives, we were granted a choice we never had before. Grace freed us from the requirement to serve sin, allowing us the opportunity to follow Christ's directives voluntarily. So as long as we do this, *we will not sin!* But as soon as you or I compromise with His mastery over us, the old master stands ready to lure us into sin.

The Grace Awakening

What good choices can you make today because of Christ's good work on the cross?

_____

_____

GOD PROMISES WISDOM

If you need wisdom, ask our generous God, and he will
give it to you. He will not rebuke you for asking.
JAMES 1:5

How do we get wisdom? According to James 1:5 we must pray for it. . . . God promises to give wisdom to us in abundance. It is essential, however, that we ask Him for it.

But praying is just one part of the process in gaining wisdom. . . . Getting wisdom is the result of mutual effort. It's a matter of working together with God in pulling off a wise lifestyle. God doesn't deliver wisdom at our door like the morning paper. Wisdom doesn't come in a neat package, like a carton of cool milk that's waiting to be opened. It's the result of a cooperative effort.

Wisdom doesn't come easily. It may start with prayer, but there's so much more. To get wisdom, we must roll up our sleeves. . . . It's like trying to find hidden treasure; it takes rugged labor. God will do His part if we'll only do ours. It's a mutual process.

Living on the Ragged Edge

What wisdom from God do you need specifically for today?

_____

_____

_____

_____

Acknowledgments

Grateful acknowledgment is made to the following publishers for permission to reprint this copyrighted material. All copyrights held by the author, Charles R. Swindoll.

Improving Your Serve (Nashville: Word, 1981).

Strengthening Your Grip (Nashville: Word, 1982).

Dropping Your Guard (Nashville: Word, 1982).

Living on the Ragged Edge (Nashville: Word, 1985).

Living Above the Level of Mediocrity (Nashville: Word, 1987).

Living Beyond the Daily Grind (Nashville: Word, 1988).

Living Beyond the Daily Grind II (Nashville: Word, 1988).

Growing Wise in Family Life (Portland: Multnomah Press, 1988).

The Grace Awakening (Nashville: Word, 1990).

Simple Faith (Nashville: Word, 1991).

Laugh Again (Nashville: Word, 1992).

The Finishing Touch (Nashville: Word, 1994).

The Mystery of God's Will (Nashville: Word, 1995).

Hope Again (Nashville: Word, 1996).

Intimacy with the Almighty (Nashville: J. Countryman, 1996).

David: A Man of Passion and Destiny (Nashville: Word, 1997).

Joseph: A Man of Integrity and Forgiveness (Nashville: Word, 1998).

Esther: A Woman of Strength and Dignity (Nashville: Word, 1999).

Moses: A Man of Selfless Dedication (Nashville: Word, 1999).

Perfect Trust (Nashville: J. Countryman, 2000).

Elijah: A Man of Heroism and Humility (Nashville: Word, 2000).

Day by Day with Charles Swindoll (Nashville: Word, 2000).

Flying Closer to the Flame (Nashville: Word, 1993).